Experiences in Relatedness: Groupwork and the Person-Centred Approach

Edited by
Colin Lago
and
Mhairi MacMillan

PCCS BOOKS
Ross-on-Wye

First published in 1999

PCCS BOOKS
Llangarron
Ross-on-Wye
Herefordshire
HR9 6PT
UK
Tel +44 (0)1989 77 07 07

**Experiences in Relatedness:
Groupwork and The Person-Centred Approach**

A CIP catalogue record for this book is available from the British Library

ISBN 1 898059 23 3

Cover design by Denis Postle.
Printed by Redwood Books, Trowbridge, Wiltshire, UK

CONTENTS

SINCE THE CHAPTERS ARE SO HEAVILY THEMED AND WELL SUB-HEADED,
A SUBJECT INDEX WAS THOUGHT TO BE LARGELY REDUNDANT.

ACKNOWLEDGEMENTS

We are more than acutely aware that we could not have written this book without the support, help and assistance of so many people. We are of course deeply indebted to all those other members of groups and workshops in which we have participated and with whom we have learned.

We have received such support in compiling this book from a very wide variety of colleagues both in the U.K. and in other countries and our more specific thanks to the authors of the chapters are recorded in the Introduction.

Our gratitude is also extended to Dr. Nat Raskin for writing the foreword to this book.

We both wish to record our considerable thanks to Christine Davison who has tirelessly facilitated the transmission of faxes, e-mails, phone messages and so on between us and the various authors.

We have been gently and patiently encouraged and supported by our publishers, Pete Sanders and Maggie Taylor-Sanders in bringing this text to fruition and to them we owe a big thank you.

Colin Lago and Mhairi MacMillan
January 1999

FOREWORD

NATHANIEL J. RASKIN

With this book, Colin Lago and Mhairi MacMillan have made a major addition to the rich fund of British contributions to person-centered literature. This volume on group work draws upon the rich experience and conceptualization of an outstanding international assemblage of theorists and practitioners of this orientation.

I feel fortunate to have experienced first-hand both the early days of 'non-directive therapy' when it was applied just to individuals and also the beginnings of the application of client-centered principles to groups. Rogers's talk on 'Some Newer Concepts of Psychotherapy' when he visited the University of Minnesota in December, 1940 and his book, 'Counseling and Psychotherapy,' which grew out of it and contained the ground-breaking verbatim account of the eight interviews which made up 'The Case of Herbert Bryan,' were based on a one-to-one helping situation. As a student at Ohio State University from 1940 to 1942, I learned how to do therapy with individuals, exclusively. This did not diminish the excitement of participating in a revolutionary new approach, where counsellors did not take case histories, use diagnostic tests, or give advice.

I was in the university library on the Sunday when Franklin D. Roosevelt spoke to our people about the attack on Pearl Harbor and the entrance of the United States into World War II. After three years of military service I resumed my graduate study with 'Dr. Rogers' at the University of Chicago in 1946. In contrast to the situation at Ohio State at the beginning of the decade I found that there was now a great deal of interest in groups. This had several sources. The University of Chicago's Counseling Center had been hired by the government to put on a training program for personal counselors employed by the Veterans' Administration and the student counselors responded to the student-centered atmosphere by sharing their personal feelings and experiences. Additionally, the staff meetings of the Counseling Center had an equalitarian mode of operating rather than a traditional authoritarian kind of governance. A third factor grew out of Carl Rogers 'ceasing to be a teacher' in his courses on counseling and psychotherapy. Another important influence was Virginia Axline's group play therapy sessions at the Counseling Center. In one of them, she quotes eight-year-old 'Herby,' who exults in the experience of his newly found self:

> . . . all of a sudden, I'm free. I'm Herb and Frankenstein and Tojo and a devil . . . I'm a great giant and a hero. I'm wonderful and I'm terrible. I'm a dope and I'm so smart . . . I'm good and I'm bad and still I'm Herby. I tell you I'm wonderful. I can be anything I want to be! (V. Axline, *Play Therapy*, New York: Ballantine Books, 1947, revised 1969, p. 19).

I started to catch up with 'Herby' when, in the late 1950s, I joined the American Academy of Psychotherapists, and was struck by how much I learned about myself in small groups which started out with the didactic purpose of learning how to do psychotherapy by demonstrating to one another the way we practiced. Gradually, over the years, we found ourselves talking less about our clients and more about ourselves. It dawned on me that this kind of group experience was something I could offer clients in the private practice I had at the time.

I had a Saturday morning schedule of four individual therapy sessions. I asked these four people if, instead of their individual hours, they would like to try meeting in a small group for four hours. Each one responded positively, and we met weekly in this new format for over a year. Later in the group's life, I proposed a weekend meeting in the country, with apparently very good results. This was the beginning of many group experiences in my clinical practice as well as my life as a clinical psychology professor, and as a workshop participant.

The work Colin Lago and Mhairi MacMillan have assembled in this book seems to lead towards the concept of community. I, too, have been fascinated by how the person-centered approach grew from the setting of a counseling office in which a client sat in a hard chair at the side of a desk and the therapist sat in another hard chair behind the desk to a group which is often quite large and seated informally in a circle. The individuals in the group may look very different and may come from many different parts of the world. To varying degrees, they are aware of the desirability of being empathic, congruent and having unconditional positive regard. They will surely live up to these ideals imperfectly. But, in my experience, this leaderless group will, despite considerable conflict and pain along the way, develop a group with its own unique life and, often, a spirit of community.

Each such experience helps distinguish this approach as a special one, one with real respect for the ability of the participants to learn and grow individually and to contribute to the evolution of the group. I believe this book will be an important source of intellectual and emotional stimulation for those interested in learning more about person-centered groups.

Nathaniel J. Raskin
January 1999

Contributors

John Barkham is a practitioner of the Person-Centred Approach in the context of higher education in England and Northern Ireland. He leads teams of subject specialists reviewing the quality of education provided by universities and colleges of higher education. This work is very much at the interface with non-person-centred organisational behaviour.

Alan Coulson was a school teacher for twenty years, then, until retirement, a senior lecturer in management. His commitment to the Person-Centred Approach was established through workshops in the 1970s. Currently he facilitates a psychology study programme for retired people . In addition to articles on person-centred groups his publications include pieces on cinema and management.

Irene Fairhurst writes: I was born in 1941 and I left my seaside home at the age of 17 to live in a community in East london where I became a volunteer youth worker and later trained to be a full-time youth and community worker. It was during this training that I discovered the work of Carl Rogers and went to my first person-centred workshop in the late 1970s.

Since then I have participated in workshops and training programmes at home and overseas and created several person-centred groups, including being co-founder of the British Association for the Person-Centred Approach, the Institute of Person-Centred Learning and recently Person-Centred Interaction.

Peter Figge PhD, Dip. Psych., is Director of the Counselling and Psychotherapy Centre for students at the University of Hamburg, Germany. Studies of Education and Sociology at Hamburg and the University of Lund, Sweden. He is a clinical psychologist with special training in client-centred psychotherapy and behaviour therapy. Peter Figge is currently working as trainer and supervisor and is a member of the PSYCHE group (Psychological Counselling in Higher Education) with

FEDORA. His special fields of interest are psychotherapy, psychotherapy research and the use of different media in counselling and psychotherapy.

Jane Hoffman, Dip. Couns., has a small private counselling practice in rural Fife, Scotland and also works with a national voluntary counselling organisation. Jane has a deep interest in the phenomenon of 'acceptance', as experienced personally in therapy and further, its extension to more general areas of human relating and negotiation.

Colin Lago is the Director of the Counselling Service at the University of Sheffield. His previous publications reflect a strong concern for people in their cultural and societal contexts, particularly in relation to transcultural settings. He previously worked as a youth worker in the East End of London and as a teacher in Jamaica.

Mhairi MacMillan has over twenty years' experience in person-centred groups. She has previously headed a university counselling service, lectured in counselling and authored a number of book chapters. Currently she works independently as a counsellor, supervisor and writer and at extending her knowledge of the mystical philosopher, Muhijiddin Ibn Al-Arabi.

Tony Merry works at the University of East London where he teaches on postgraduate counselling and psychotherapy courses. He is also a consultant and occasional contributor to the work of the Institute for Person-Centred Learning. He is author of a number of books and journal articles in person-centred psychology.

Peggy Natiello, Ph.D is a psychotherapist in private practice, consultant, and faculty mentor in the Prescott College Masters Program in Counseling Psychology and in The Indepth Training Program in the Person-Centered Approach. She lives in Sedona, Arizona, a place of astounding beauty and inspiration, which helps her to overcome the anxiety caused by writing.

Ruth Sanford writes: From my mother, a loving disciplinarian, and my father, a failure who accepted me unconditionally, I learned to love people and knew I had a place in this world. At 12 I declined confirmation because I did not believe in original sin and have been a troublemaker ever since. Since 1975 I have facilitated workshops with Carl Rogers and others in many countries around the world. At age 92, despite catastrophic loss of eyesight I continue to write and facilitate workshops.

John Keith Wood, Ph.D graduated in mathematics and engineering before turning to a career in psychology. For fifteen years, he was a companion of Carl R. Rogers, contributing to understanding the psychology of large groups. In addition to continuing this interest, Dr. Wood lives on and works a citrus farm in Brazil.

INTRODUCTION

How this book came into being has now been somewhat obscured by our own closeness to and passion for this project. Our attempt, therefore, to write a brief introductory history is in great danger of faulty memories, fictionalising and perhaps some exaggeration! Nevertheless we hope that some personal reflections will enable the reader to understand our motivation in bringing such a volume together, the first, we believe, on the Person-Centred Approach to Group Work since Rogers wrote *Encounter Groups* in 1970. This fact, that many groups and workshops were meeting, and little was being recorded in book form, was our main starting point. The idea has been with us for at least five years. It has been a long time coming into print.

Our history in groups
Mhairi
Mhairi's experience of groupwork began with participation in an in-service course related to her job as a Guidance Teacher in a Scottish secondary school. The course was entitled 'Helping Interviews and Groupwork Skills'. Leadership of the course had just been taken on by a psychology lecturer recently returned from a year at the Center for Studies of the Person in La Jolla, California. His name was Dave Mearns.

In the same year (1976), she first took part in the Facilitator Development Institute workshops, described by John Barkham later in the book. The purpose of these workshops was stated as giving 'experience and theory in the facilitation of groups, (FDI brochure). About the same time, FDI workshops were being convened in Holland, Germany and France. The times were right for these enterprises, 'encounter' was in vogue, and innovation was still possible in such fields as education, social work and counselling, then still in its infancy. Mhairi writes:

> I had never had such a sense of freedom as I had experienced at the
> York workshop. Talk about the expansion of the self-concept!
> Certainly, I was hungry for the social closeness available and found

the mix of nationalities, ages and personalities exhilarating. More importantly, although I had not read Carl Rogers (I had heard of his work and ideas) I had the experience of being accepted for myself, of being listened to, of being a listener myself, of not being responsible for a single other person (I was a lone parent with two children). I was experiencing the Person Centred Approach in action.

By 1980, after attendance at the intervening annual workshops, Mhairi had been asked to take on the role of an 'apprentice facilitator' and there experienced the pressures not only of facilitating but of the sense that the original freshness of the core staff team was proving difficult to sustain. (This phenomenon has been noted in the psychoanalytic large group literature as well as referred to in the chapters by John Barkham and John K. Wood.)

Two specially convened workshops were of particular significance for Mhairi: the 1981 meeting in Zinal, Switzerland and the La Jolla International Program in Istanbul, Turkey, 1988. She has also attended Cross-Cultural Communication workshops, International Forums and International Conferences on Client-Centred and Experiential Psychotherapy – of which, in 1991, both editors were on the organising committee.

Colin

Colin's original professional background was in youth and community work, the training for which had been predominantly set within seminar and tutorial group settings. Soon after qualification, he embarked upon an in-service course in London on authority and role in organisations. The experience proved so difficult that he withdrew, only attending half of the course! The dramatic contrast between the one year group experience of his training course (which had largely been very educational and supportive) and this short course, (which had proved extremely aggressive, confrontational and not at all supportive!) was considerable, needless to say, and distressing.

Early group theory (Bennis and Shepard, 1973) hypothesising the stages of development of groups (forming, storming, norming, performing and reforming) might simply account for the aggressive group dynamics experienced by Colin in this latter group in its early weeks of existence, being described as in the 'storming' phase. Rogers's hypotheses concerning the conditions necessary for conducive communication to occur, whether in therapy, in the classroom or in groupwork, i.e. the establishment of 'climate' within group settings, have thus always made great sense to us.

Having qualified and then gained employment as a counsellor in the late 70s, Colin attended his first large group workshop in Hungary in 1983. 300 participants, over 20 nationalities, seven days duration, all experiential – are just some brief descriptors of what proved to be an extraordinary experience. Attendance at subsequent 'Cross-Cultural' workshops (as they were known), in the following years led on to Colin being invited to be a facilitating staff member at the Paris workshop (1988), the organiser of the Sheffield workshop (1989), and part of the facilitating team in Pforzheim, Germany (1990) and Modra-Harmonia (in what was then Czechoslovakia) in 1991.

Writing about groups

As a result of both editors having been on the facilitating teams of the above Cross-Cultural workshops, various papers were co-written and published. (MacMillan and Lago, 1993, 1996). Our interests in recent years have thus been focused on the application of the PCA to large group work, believing that knowledge gained from this field could be disseminated, through application, to the establishment and enhancement of community, wherever that community existed (see Lago, 1994). At the same time, however, we have both continued to have small group experiences in counsellor training groups, student workshops and therapy groups.

Group activity in the person-centred approach

We cannot attempt to give a comprehensive list of group activities. This would have to cover all five continents – Africa, America (North and South), Australia, Asia and Europe, and many different types of activity; for example, counselling training, other learning programmes, therapy groups, support groups, teacher training, personal and professional development groups. Distinguished practitioners and writers on groupwork include Goff Barrett-Lennard in Australia (see Barrett-Lennard, 1994, 1998) Leif Braaten in Norway (e.g. Braaten, 1998), Germain Lietaer in Belgium (e.g. Lietaer et al, 1996) in Portugal, Joao Marques-Teixera (Marques-Teixera et al, 1996) and Shoji Murayama in Japan (Murayama and Nakata,1996). The network of support groups known as 'Fukuoka Human Relations Community' grew out of a seminar led by Shoji Murayama on Carl Rogers's writings and 'began during the student riots in the 1960s as an attempt to deal with Japan's oppressive, hierarchical society' (Murayama, 1996). We had hoped to include some of Professor Murayama's current writing in this book and much regret that we have been unable to do so.

One of the first group activities was the La Jolla Program, which still runs annually on the campus of the University of California at San Diego. A current convener, Will Stilwell, writes of the program:

> 'Encounter' is a good word for what we offer at the La Jolla Program because we encounter surprising aspects of ourselves and others in the sometimes sweet, and sometimes rough and tumble, verbal and emotional exchanges we experience.
>
> We offer an apprenticeship for the trainee to experience and be able to work from the 'inside-out' conviction that each person's life is best measured and cared for from inside that person's world . . . We offer an apprenticeship in leaving one's known world with a full heart, ready to encounter what is unknown in the other.
>
> (Stilwell, 1998)

Another meeting with a long history is the Warm Springs workshop convened by Jerold Bozarth. A participant has written:

> So what is it I expect to happen this year in Warm Springs? I expect that every day the community, or 95% of it will meet in a large group for a few hours. I expect that some boredom, conflict, resolution, more conflict, tears, intense silence, laughter, questions, answers, questions without answers, judgements, questions about being non-judgemental, questions about why we are wasting so much time will all occur.
>
> And I own them as my expectations. Nobody is there to live up to my expectations, I can assure you. I remember one woman last time asking me just why did I have to talk so much? She enjoyed the periodic silences which we all shared from time to time. Her expectations collided with mine and we both survived.
>
> I loved it last time. Every night I would go to bed later than the night before, until the last night I think I retired about three hours before the first meeting of the next day.
>
> (Blanchard, 1999)

More examples: Small, independent encounter groups in Chambery, Geneva and Annecy; support group for male counsellors in Glasgow; groups in social work training at the University South Africa; support group for serving teachers in Flanders; the Pajaro Group with the goal of bringing the person-centred approach into business and organisations and to influence social change; groups run by the British Association for the Person-Centred Approach; workshops and encounter groups run by Person-Centred Approach International (GB).

Groups are, of course, an everyday phenomena for most human beings. We live, socialise and work, to a great extent, in groups. Perhaps a more formal concept of a group is that it consists of three or more people together with a common purpose, which may be unspoken or even non-conscious. Despite this somewhat everyday exposure to groups of one form and another, a consciously intentional gathering of individuals to encounter, to be therapeutic, to explore relationships and to learn occurs less often. Groups have an enormous potential to promote learning, to help and to heal. Sadly, unfortunately, they also have the capacity to induce fear, to scapegoat, to annihilate, etc.

> There was a time when crowds and mobs seemed so different from the individual's daily behaviour that some tangible interpersonal linking or 'extra-individual' phenomena seemed to be the obvious explanation. Thus arose the notion of a kind of collective consciousness or group mind. Le Bon (1895) a sociologist-philosopher struck by the difference between the emotional and irrational quality of a person's actions in a crowd and their behaviour in ordinary surroundings, felt that a kind of hypnotic trance engendered by the crowd must be the explanation. He believed

> crowds might release deep and dark passions within the individual
> and that mob leaders worked their influence through emotion rather
> than reason.
>
> (Davis,1969: 2)

The very principles of the person centred approach are so contrary to these notions of the release of deep and dangerous passion by mob leaders wreaking emotional influence! Nevertheless, great emotion and energy can be generated in group settings and one of our concerns in this volume is to contribute to modes and styles of participant and facilitator practice that support the other rather than denigrate, seek to understand rather than judge, respect rather than demean, in short, to love rather than hate. Perhaps what is most important is that so-called negative emotions become open to transformation by their expression and acceptance within the group. For example, an expression of 'hate' such as described in chapter 1, does not remain charged with the energy of hatred once it has been outed. This is summed up also in the subtitle of the psychoanalytic book on large groups, *Koinonia: From Hate ,Through Dialogue, to Culture in the Large Group* (de Mare et al, 1991).

The authors
In our vision for this book we were keen to include as wide a range of topic and authorship as possible. The writers actually represented in the book are from Brazil, England, Germany, Scotland and the United States of America. Yet we know that we have barely begun to tap the potentially rich resource of writing on groups. We know, not only because of those writers whom we approached, but were for various reasons unable to provide a chapter at this time, but also from the number and quality of people engaged in group work, that another volume such as this could easily be filled.

Style and language
The chapters differ considerably in writing style. Compare, for example, Peter Figge's chapter on research with Ruth Sanford's on diversity. The former represents a succinct presentation of research findings supported by tables, figures and diagrams. In the latter chapter Ruth, because of vision impairment, has composed her chapter through dialogue with, and dictation to, her support colleagues. Her style is personal and intimate, and the intimacy is extended by the brief autobiographical sketches written by other staff members of the diversity workshops. Also, some of the authors were writing in their second or third language, a formidable feat in itself. Where styles of expression are unusual to you we ask you to work at uncovering the meanings intended as these authors surely had to work to write these chapters. In reading each chapter, one becomes aware of the very extensive and long-term exposure most of the authors have had to their particular fields of application. Some of the reflections and learnings they share with us, though they may appear simple and tentative, are borne out of very

considerable experience in groups themselves and from subsequent systematic reflection over time.

The chapters
The chapters are presented in the following sections:
1.Historical and contemporary overview
2.Training and development
3.Research
4.Applications
5.Large groups and workshops

One or two chapters could have been included within different headings (e.g. Peggy Natiello's chapter could have been fitted into 'applications'). Nevertheless, we hope this structure provides a more detailed breakdown of the contents. Several authors were unable to present their scripts in time for this volume. Consequently, the section on Research, for example, contains only one chapter. As we note later in this introduction, a possible second volume is under consideration and these authors will then be included.

Historical and Contemporary Overview
Chapter 1. Ruth Sanford's *A Brief History of My Experience of the Development of Small and Large Group Work in the Person-Centered Approach* tells of her experiences from the 1970s onwards with Carl Rogers in Mexico, Europe, South Africa and the Soviet Union. She lists a number of significant learnings from their work in groups and illustrates each learning from specific workshops, in a frank and acute manner. She completes the chapter by citing various colleagues who are attempting to bring the principles derived from PCA to different contemporary and contextual settings, in the belief that such attempts may bring about positive social change.

Chapter 2. Here, we (the editors) look at *PCA Groups: Past, Present . . . and Future?* We describe some key programmes and workshops starting over roughly the last 20 years; and how, inspired by our own interest in large groups and by the encouragement of colleagues, especially John K. Wood, we organised a series of seminars on this topic. Thereafter the Sedona large group experiment is briefly considered. Possibly the most significant development in the last ten years – the burgeoning of counselling training – is analysed in respect of its impact on large group meetings.

Training and Development
Chapter 3, Group Work in Client-centred Counsellor Training. Irene Fairhurst and Tony Merry take the theme of the role of the group in the context of counsellor training, where it is a training and testing ground for 'the creation of the facilitative climate of Rogers' therapeutic attitudes'. They examine some of the dilemmas of

the facilitator who is also a trainer, including issues of power and the need for facilitator restraint. They give a voice to the trainees by including some of their comments. As co-directors of the Institute for Person Centred Learning in London, their experience with training and other groups has been extensive and their chapter provides ample evidence of this.

Chapter 4, Sexism, Gender Dynamics and the Person-centered Approach. Sexism and gender dynamics are the complex oppressive social phenomena that Peggy Natiello addresses in her chapter. Her introductory pages provide a very comprehensive account of definitions, female-male relations and a consideration of consequences of sex-role stereotyping. Peggy, with her colleague Curtis Graf ran PCA based groups for 11 years, inviting dialogue on these issues. The second half of the chapter reveals some experiences and personal learnings from this wide array of experiencing.

Chapter 5. Experiencing Diversity. We have to record a special note of thanks to Ruth Sanford, who, at 91, produced two chapters both on time. This chapter, on working with diversity, represents one of the leading edges of person-centred group work at this time. Traditional person-centred groups have often taken place with participants who have had the advantages of location (e.g. universities), opportunity (e.g. availability of time) and financial support (to afford the fees, travel, etc.). The Diversity workshops have genuinely striven to be inclusive of all potential participants.

The brochure for the 1998 Experiencing Diversity workshop reads as follows:
> Come join us in a celebration of Diversity . . , a place where a group of people who have ranged in age from teens to nineties learn from and with each other. Here you will find individuals from a variety of life situations, cultures and backgrounds . . . including but not limited to persons with disabilities . . . both visible and not, people who are gay, lesbian, bisexual, asexual . . . agnostic, atheist, Buddhist, Christian, Islamic and Jewish . . . people of various colours and shades, people who speak more than one language, and people who don't. People with and without formal education who come to share the school of life, people who have money to spare and people who don't.

Her account of these workshops represents a timely initiative in the person-centred world and indeed in the world in general.

Research
Chapter 6 is a research report by Peter Figge, *Client-centred Psychotherapy in groups: Understanding the Influence of the Client-Therapist Relationship on Therapy Outcome*. It is also the only piece in the book which focusses on group psychotherapy. This is a succinct and impressive account of research results

gathered over ten years of conducting group psychotherapy for students at Hamburg University and associated colleges. The research offers clear evidence that, on a variety of measures, significant improvement is experienced by most participants. Amongst other important points, he provides research evidence to support the hypothesis that the importance of (facilitator) empathy being offered is rooted in the perception of therapist congruence. This chapter provides us with a very valuable contribution because of its systematic research conducted over such a long time.

Applications
Chapter 7. A Person-centred Approach to the Facilitation of Citizens' Juries – a Recent Development in Public Consultation is a delightful and inspiring account of a very important, innovative, democratic consultation process. This descriptive chapter introduces us to 'citizen's juries' and describes how Jane's experience of (and belief in) the person-centred approach was used by her and her colleagues in facilitating the jury members' own explorations of the key community issues they had been charged with considering. This exciting initiative is one that could be applied to so many settings and in a range of different countries.

Large Groups and Workshops
Chapter 8. John Barkham's *FDI (Britain) Workshops* is an account of the Facilitator Development Institute International Workshops which for some time provided the only independently-organised, person-centred residential large group workshops in the UK. His observations on the role of facilitators are most pertinent as is his exploration of the issue of power. Interestingly, power emerges in several of the other chapters as an issue of concern and challenge to facilitatiors and participants. Who has it? Who exercises it? How is it handled? How is it applied? These and many other questions surrounding power are necessarily both concerning and worthy of considerable exploration by anyone wishing to work in person-centred groups.

Chapter 9. Toward an Understanding of Large Group Dialogue and its Implications, is written by one who was involved with Carl Rogers in large group workshops from their beginnings and who has continued to reflect critically on the 'phenomenon of group' right up until this present moment. We have both been most grateful for all the support and enthusiasm for our interest in group phenomena generously extended by John K. Wood over many years now. Colin recollects reading the first draft of John's chapter sitting on a rock in the Arizona desert whilst at the Sedona workshop and becoming so absorbed that he almost missed the following group session! John's chapter is a very carefully considered synthesis of acute observations, careful and precise reflections, studied attention to exactly what constitutes the PCA in this arena and wide-ranging references and allusions to work carried out in parallel fields of endeavour. It fully deserves the expression 'tour de force'.

Chapter 10. In *Experiences of Separateness and Unity in Person-centred Groups*, Alan Coulson looks at the phenomenon of awareness within some participants in large group meetings of their intrinsic connection with others in a unity that transcends their separate individual concerns. Alan's twenty-year experience of large groups, along with a scholarly reading of contemporary literature on human consciousness, informs his view of how the large group process may become one of bringing about a change of awareness from that of the conditioned, separate self-experiencing and behaviour to the unconditional 'experiencing more fully the present moment and the unity of the Self'.

In Summation
This book does not claim to provide a comprehensive coverage of the full range of person-centred approach group-work – far from it, and doubtless the omissions outnumber the inclusions in terms of quantity. However, we believe that the quality of the chapters that we have been able to include will both interest and inspire readers to initiate or continue group activities and, especially, to reflect on them critically and in further writing. Certainly this is our intention.

References

Barrett-Lennard, G. T. (1994) 'Toward a Person-Centered Theory of Community' *J of Humanistic Psychology* 34, 3: 62–86.

Barrett-Lennard, G. T. (1998) *Carl Rogers' Helping System*. London: Sage.

Bennis, W. G. and Shepard, H. A. (1973) 'A Theory of Group Development' In R. T. Golembiewski and A Blumberg (eds) *Sensitivity Training and the Laboratory Approach*. Itasca Illinois: Peacock.

Blanchard, P. (1999) E-mail communication.

Braaten, L. J. (1998) A person-centred perspective on leadership and team-building; in B. Thorne and E. Lambers (eds) *Person-centred Therapy: A European Perspective*. London: Sage.

Davis, J.H. (1969) *Group Performance*. Reading, Mass: Addison Wesley.

Lago, C. O. (1994) 'Therapy for a Masturbatory Society: the Need for Connectedness', *Counselling*, 5, 2.

Le Bon, G. (1895) *Psychologie des foules*. Paris: G. Olean.

Leitaer, G, and Dierick, P. (1996) Client-centered Group Psychotherapy in Dialogue with Other Orientations: Commonality and Specificity. In R. Hutterer, G. Pawlowsky, P. Schmid and R. Stipsits (eds) *Client-centered and Experiential Psychotherapy: a Paradigm in Motion*, Frankfurt: Peter Lang.

MacMillan, M. I. and Lago, C. O. (1993) 'Large Groups: Critical Reflections and Some Concerns, in *The Person-centered Approach and Cross-Cultural Communication: an International Review*, vol 2.

MacMillan, M. I. and Lago, C. O. (1996) The Facilitation of Large Groups: Participants' Experiences of Facilitative Moments. In R. Hutterer, G. Pawlowsky, P. Schmid and R. Stipsits (eds) *Client-centered and Experiential*

Psychotherapy: a Paradigm in Motion, Frankfurt: Peter Lang.

Marques-Teixera, J., Pires de Carvalho, M.M., Moreira, A.M. and Pinho, C. (1996) 'Group Effect'? Implication of the Barrett-Lennard Inventory on 5 Individual Group Types. In R. Hutterer, G. Pawlowsky, P. Schmid and R. Stipsits (eds) *Client-centered and Experiential Psychotherapy: a Paradigm in Motion*, Frankfurt: Peter Lang.

Murayama, S. (1996) Personal communication.

Rogers, C.R. (1970) *Encounter Groups*. London: Penguin.

Stilwell, W. (1998) Personal communication.

AN HISTORICAL AND CONTEMPORARY OVERVIEW

A Brief History of My Experience of the Development of Small and Large Group Work in the Person-Centred Approach

1

Ruth Sanford

Preface

I wish to acknowledge the assistance of Ed Bodfish without whom this chapter would not have been completed. It was necessary for him to review the notes which I kept for each of the more than 100 workshops in which I have facilitated or assisted in facilitating, in order for me to obtain the information needed to quote directly from notes made during the workshops themselves. He also did valuable editing and offered suggestions for including content.

Cheryl Desrosiers typed my notes and journals and transcribed them so that they were available for future use. Without her dedicated assistance I could not have kept accurate pertinent records of my experience in both large and small groups.

I recognize the contribution made by Diane Cheeseman, a friend who changed my awareness and therefore influenced my perspective. When I told her that I had lost all but two per cent of my vision, her reply was, 'You may have lost all but two per cent of your eyesight but I see nothing wrong with your vision.' She gave me perspective and encouragement at a critical time in my life.

I wish to acknowledge the continued support and encouragement of my daughter, Mei-Mei Sanford, who added comments that were of genuine assistance in producing a finished copy.

It seems important before discussing the application of the Person Centered Approach in large and small groups to define the term briefly. Carl Rogers stated that it was his experience that when genuineness or realness, acceptance or unconditional positive regard, and empathy – which includes deep listening – are present, then positive change and growth are most likely, to take place.[1] He further

---

[1] See Carl Rogers (1980) *A Way of Being*, Boston: Houghton Mifflin. Chapter 6, 'The Foundations of a Person-Centered Approach'.

referred to these conditions as creating a climate conducive to positive change. The foundation of the PCA is a trust in the self-actualizing tendency. Carl Rogers went on to say he believed this same tendency to self-actualize is present in the universe and is known as the formative tendency. There is in every organism, including humans, an underlying flow of movement toward constructive fulfilment of its inherent possibilities, a natural tendency toward growth. It can be thwarted but not destroyed without destroying the whole organism (Rogers 1977). With this background we can proceed to the history of my own personal experience in planned intensive PCA groups, both large and small, in many countries.[2]

Personal reflections

In 1973, the year of my retirement, after 18 years as counselor, researcher, and administrator of counseling services in public schools in West Hempstead, Long Island, I had my first direct exposure to the PCA as it evolved over the adult life of Carl Rogers. I immediately had a knowing that here was my professional home. That knowing has remained constant. Out of it has grown what I shall call the history of my experience of small and large groups in the PCA. As I looked back on the 25 years I was amazed as I became aware that I had been involved in more than 100 such groups in which I had been a participant or a facilitator, many of them as co-facilitator with Carl Rogers.

Our work together took us from the US to Mexico, Europe, South Africa, the Soviet Union, and many other places. In yet other workshops we were members of a facilitating staff. Since Carl's death on February 4, 1987, I have continued as a counselor in private practice, facilitator in groups, and invited facilitator and presenter in the US, Europe, Russia, and South Africa.

I have experienced short term groups ranging downward from 6000 to 200–300. Are these large groups? The length of time ranged from an hour and a half to two days. Do you need a longer time to be effective? What is the difference between a large group and a small group? Is it a matter of numbers alone? Or is it a matter of the degree of intimacy that is experienced, so that a group of 200 can feel as safe as a group of 40?

A group large or small is likely to begin with tentative exchanges, gestures at getting acquainted, and may pass through sharp differences, even chaos, until one or more people may make known a desire to hear everyone. At that point participants usually begin to listen to one another and the group tends to move in a more positive direction. As I review the record of many intensive groups I can say with assurance that this process is representative of both large and small groups.

In groups from 5 or 10 up to the 50s it is possible for a higher degree of intimacy

---

[2] For more general history I shall refer to two excellent sources of the earlier history of the evolution of Client-Centered Therapy to the Person Centered Approach in planned intensive groups from 1946 to the early 70s:
a) Carl Rogers (1970) *On Encounter Groups*, New York, Harper and Row.
b) Howard Kirschenbaum (1979). *On Becoming Carl Rogers*, New York, Delacorte.

to develop than in a group of 200. It would be impossible in a group of 600 or 1000 to reach the degree of intimacy of a very small group of 5–50, but positive change can still take place, as attested by the Witwatersrand, Johannesburg meeting of 1982.

In Guadalajara we adjourned from the large general community meeting of 1600–1800 in the municipal auditorium to meet with small groups on campus. When Carl and I arrived we found the 'small group' was 200!

This is also the meeting where Carl made a fairly lengthy statement, which the translator then proceeded to handle. The translation went on for a very long time. I don't know Spanish and said to myself, 'Hmmm, it must take longer to say things in Spanish.' When the translator finished, she asked Carl, 'How was that?' Carl knew a little Spanish and replied, 'Oh fine, and I liked your speech too.'

My challenge in the writing of this chapter is to distil not only the experiences but also the learnings, to acknowledge not only the ways in which the work has been effective, but also to recognize the shortcomings. I do not want to be understood as saying the PCA is the only way to effect positive change. It is the way I know best and in which I feel most at home.

Learnings

I should like to list some general principles that will be in effect throughout this paper. First, I believe the only reality we have is our perception of reality. Therefore my perception will vary from many who have also experienced groups to which I shall refer. Second, the authority to determine what has been helpful or harmful in the therapeutic relationship or in a group rests with the client or the participant. Therefore I shall rely heavily on direct quotations from participants in the groups, supplemented by my own journals or my memory of how the overall process developed in a given group. Third, I shall wherever possible select details from my written record of the time rather than my memory, which I have learned can play tricks on me. It tends to remember the things I want to remember and to forget the things I want to forget. Fourth, it has been my experience that if you can establish communication across lines of conflict, difference, or estrangement between members of a group or between the estranged parts of an individual as in psychotherapy, then healing or positive change almost inevitably will take place.

After being as real and open as I can be at this moment about my present state of awareness, I shall state some learnings in which I feel confidence. I want it to be understood that I am trying to be very honest about this.

The learnings are:
- Our only reality is our perception of reality.
- It is important to be totally present.
- Dissension in the planning group is mirrored in the workshop.
- Harmony in the planning group is mirrored in the workshop.
- Make it clear that you want to hear each person.
- It is important that someone provide the facilitative conditions.
- Deep understanding of the PCA on the part of the facilitators is important.

While I have illustrated each learning with a workshop(s), each workshop exemplified many points.

My mind is teeming with the words of those who have found healing and wholeness in large and small groups.

Our only reality is our perception of reality – Dublin 1985

An apt illustration of the premise 'Our only reality is our perception of reality' is the Dublin workshop of 1985. I am choosing Dublin because it is a workshop rich in the number of comments of participants written at the time. John, Eddie, Theresa, Ursula, Colin, Carl and I all had very different perceptions of Dublin. With the exception of the acknowledgment that it was a complex and difficult group of 160 people extending over seven days there seems to have been little agreement on what occurred or its importance.

John: It was funny, even hilarious at times. It was draining, annoying and overpowering. It was frustrating just to be there, but you did not want to leave. You might miss something, though it did not appear as if we were heading anywhere fast. His dozen or so lieutenants [the staff] spread out among the group of 160 which surrounded him. They were endeavouring to let this workshop get going in the best possible non-directive way. They misjudged it slightly a couple of times and were almost eaten. God! It was difficult not knowing where you were going and having absolutely no structure or agenda (though there were personal expectations or agendas) to guide you, but the uncertainty and freedom grew more interesting and inviting all the time and nobody was taking that away from 'The Group'.

What about cross-cultural communication? After all that is what it was supposed to be about! Well, at the end of a shared, intense, demanding and stimulating week, when national identities were beginning to take second place to an overall, if tentative, bond and individual connections and friendships, it certainly seemed that the range of emotions and feelings we had gone through had done more to highlight, at the personal level at least, our similarities rather than our differences.

Eddie and *Theresa*, the local hosts of the workshop reported: We have had an abundance of positive, supportive, and encouraging letters from persons who attended the workshop. I find it extremely encouraging for future efforts.

Ursula: To be quite fair, my first disappointed reaction to the workshop was due to a large gap in communication between myself and the writers of the advertising brochure. I expected to learn directly about skills and methods of the Client or Person-Centered Approach, and how to use them to greater effect in my work as a counselor. . . to concentrate not only on the words used, but also on the gestures, facial expressions, tone of voice, in order to understand the real feelings or distress behind the dry words. In the large group of 100–150 participants, this was not physically possible.

I was finally disillusioned by the superb showmanship of some of the participants, as they threaded their lines through the genuinely expressed fears and hopes of the others.

For me the last straw was when in some of the smaller groups, I heard repeated word for word, the eloquent lyrical phrases of self-revelation used in the larger group, and what had sounded like an echo of psychic pain, through repetition became a carefully rehearsed plea for attention. But by now my tolerance had vanished and so had I.

Colin: A French poet is attributed with the quotation 'when I hate, I think' (reference unknown). During the conference in Ireland, after several days of heated exchange that seemed without humour or joy, one participant stood up and said to another, 'I hate you.' 'You cannot say you hate,' became the essence of several rapid responses. [In reply] the original speaker said, 'Do not deny me my hate. It is mine. I feel it. It is what I do with it that matters. It makes me think.' This very profound and heated interchange had enormous ripple effects for the rest of the conference.

Somehow, inside the large group, the processes were significantly effected and soon after, the group began to take much more time to listen and respond to each other. The rapid rat-tat-tat of disconnected speeches gave way to more exploratory responses, more silences and different levels of communication occurred.

Carl: People seemed to listen to one another. People also spoke of how valuable the workshop had been to them. Although it has been a very difficult and struggling workshop, I think most people feel they have profited.

For myself, I feel that this has been a very painful, conflicted, angry, sometimes deceitful workshop, but that it has gradually come to a good conclusion, with a broadened understanding of different groups, individuals, and cultures and an increased acceptance of personal differences. It has not, I feel, been easy for anyone. Whatever degree of improved communication has been achieved, it has been a hard won-gain.

Ruth: I will give a quick overview without giving attention to details. My impression of the hate encounter was that Tony had been sincere. It was the first open statement of the tension that existed between North and South, between Protestant and Catholic Ireland, tension that undoubtedly had effects on the entire workshop. I saw the intervention of Chuck Devonshire when he stood up as in readiness to prevent physical violence between Tony and Willy. This encounter's effect was very powerful, probably the most significant few moments of the workshop.

In PC workshops there were usually calls for and resistance to the formation of small groups. In this workshop there seemed to be an insistence by many on staying in the large group. Without a general consensus by all participants, small groups began to form until the large group numbered about 20 or 25. Insisting on remaining in the large meeting room, the large group became a small group.

I recall that I arranged to meet with three educationally-limited Irish mothers who expressed their need for help with their problems of everyday living. I invited them and anyone who wished to join us to meet as a small group. A group of about ten men and women joined us for two or three small group sessions. It became a very intimate and, I believe, growthful experience.

Carl gave a half-hour demonstration therapy with a client. At the time there were strong expressions of interest and the feeling that the session had value not only to the client but also to the observing participants. Nowhere in the evaluations written after the workshop was the demonstration interview mentioned except by the client

It is important to be totally present – Tbilisi 1986

I have found that when I can enter into a group ready to be as completely present and acceptant, even with those with whom I differ, as is humanly possible for me to be, I am most likely to be effective as a facilitator. If there is some reason I cannot be totally present, I will try to make my feelings known in a way that will be least hurtful. I find that if I have unexpressed negative feelings, I cannot be entirely present. Let me illustrate with an experience in Tbilisi, Georgia in the Soviet Union in 1986.

In a kind of rhythm, theoretical questions – some inquisitive, some critical, some purely provocative – alternated with disclosures of deep personal experiences. This pattern continued throughout the second day and into the third. I noticed that theoretical or philosophical questions were directed to Carl, never to me, which was quite different from all of our previous experience. That evening I spoke to Carl about my feeling of unease and expressed my feeling that I must make my uneasiness known in the group if I were to remain actively engaged, because I had sensed that I was withdrawing somewhat on the third day. Carl replied, 'I would hope you could make that feeling known.'

The following morning, I told the group how I had been feeling. I didn't know what it signified, I said, but I felt very much a part of the group at all times except when theoretical or philosophical questions came up. I wondered whether it was because Carl was a renowned psychologist, a person of prominence, or whether it was because he was a man. In Georgia perhaps the man was looked to for the intellectual, the factual, and the theoretical, rather than the woman. Whatever it was, I would be interested in knowing. I did not want anyone to make an apology, but I said, 'It took me until late in life to appreciate my brain, that I have a brain, and I don't want to give that up. So, I feel that I have been honest with you about my feeling. Now I can become more whole-heartedly a member of the group.' The reaction was the first really intense, involved discussion of men-women relationships that we had had in all of the Soviet Union. At the end of our discussion, the Director of the Institute (who had requested permission to become a member of the group) spoke up very thoughtfully, saying he had not been aware of his lack of appreciation for the women on his staff, that he felt he had been holding within himself a double standard, and that he intended to pay more attention to the accomplishments, contributions, and work of the women of his staff. He seemed close to tears when he said, 'That includes my wife' (who was present as a participant).

Irina was my interpreter in Moscow in 1986. She had done a great deal of significant work but had always subordinated herself to her superior. On the way to Tbilisi in Georgia after Moscow we said to her 'We hope you will become a participant in this workshop rather than continue as a translator.' She did and at the end of the day in which much time had been spent on men-women relationships, Irina suddenly stood up and, flinging her arms wide, she shouted, 'Hullo, Irina!' In 1998 she said to me she had never felt such freedom as at that moment.

Dissension in the planning group is mirrored in the workshop

I have learned that when dissension and unresolved conflicts exist within the facilitative staff members, the intensive group experience will reflect the same lack of clear communication and harmony. The tone of a workshop is directly determined by the quality of the relationship between those who plan and facilitate it, for want of a better term, known as 'the staff'. If, on the other hand, the staff shows the characteristics of a close knit community capable of resolving its own conflicts and dealing constructively with its differences, the intensive group they facilitate is most likely to become a positive growth experience for most participants.

At a workshop in upper New York State the staff was sharply divided. The workshop struggled for two weeks in spite of some last minute reconciliations on the part of participants and closed with many negative feelings unaddressed.

The next and last workshop facilitated by the same staff is reported to have ended in chaos and a feeling of bewilderment or despair on the part of many participants and at least one staff member. Yet even when there is dissension amongst the staff a few participants may still benefit.

Another illustration of the results of unresolved tension among members of the planning/facilitating group involves a workshop held at a university in greater New York. Unlike the first workshops mentioned, I was a member of the planning/ facilitative group, which numbered about 12. It consisted not only of the facilitators of a learning program in which participants enrolled for a semester or a year, but also students from the program. It was decided to include them all on the facilitating staff. It was an experiment that resulted in the largest number of facilitators proportionately we ever tried. The participants in the workshop totalled about 100. It was designed to take place in two parts of four days each. There was a long period of hesitancy on the part of the 'staff' as to how to begin. Participants became restless and angry. Conversations arose in different parts of the room. This atmosphere seemed to exist in varying degrees throughout the first four days. Some participants found stimulation and excitement in the confrontations, but many left. In spite of various attempts on the part of the staff to bring the group together, it ended with many participants leaving with feelings of hurt, of being deeply wounded or angry. I know some still carry the results of those wounds to this day. It seems that not only the lack of essential harmony but also the number included in the staff resulted in minimizing benefits to the larger group. This is not a criticism of the learning program, which undoubtedly was very effective for many participants over a period of years.

Fortunately Part II, to which everyone participating in Part I was invited, followed in a different part of the building after a break of three days. The group numbered about 40. It was facilitated by two experienced facilitators.

Considerable time was taken to discuss the principles and philosophy of the PCA with emphasis on the questions and comments of the participants. On request one of the facilitators conducted a counseling session, which resulted in lively discussion. The fourth day ended with the free participation of members of the group in a wide variety of communication including music, movement to music, relaxation, dancing and some of the deepest sharing of the eight days. Several of the participants remarked there had been room for their creative selves. It seems as if it was a time for healing and renewal for most of those involved. While I wish to let the experience speak for itself, I do want to observe that in Part II the emphasis changed from *what should the staff be doing?* to *what are the participants here for?* There was also a second chance for healing.

It seems strange as I look back that the same design for planning and facilitation was employed at a one day workshop in another university in New York City two years later. Carl Rogers had been featured in the publicity and brochures. Members of the learning group who varied somewhat from the earlier workshop were seated on stage as part of the facilitative 'staff'. Professors from the university came with high expectations, and several persons with long-time interests in the PCA also attended. Carl was late because of a car breakdown and considerable concern and anxiety had already taken hold when he arrived. The audience clearly wanted to hear a presentation from Carl but he deferred in favor of the group on-stage. The result was a day in which no one was genuinely happy. At a meeting of the staff afterwards there were sharp interchanges but no resolution. There was a feeling of disappointment and unrealized anticipation. A few members of the audience lingered and expressed their enthusiasm for what had taken place calling it 'stimulating' and 'fascinating'. As far as I know the design was not used again.

In a group in which I was a member of the facilitative staff some sharp conflicts had developed among the facilitators. Although they maintained a history of closeness on most issues, it was the only workshop of a series of four that ended in unaddressed or unresolved feelings on the part of several participants and staff members. Having worked together in other workshops over a period of time our connection was sufficiently strong that after the workshop we reached a consensus to concentrate on our learnings rather than on our past pain, struggle, and differences. There is a great deal of benefit gained from working together over the years.

Harmony in the planning group is mirrored in the workshop

This learning is illustrated in the Witwatersrand 1986 and the Moscow and Tbilisi 1986 workshops described in other sections of this chapter.

Make it clear that you want to hear – Witwatersrand 1982

This was our first visit to South Africa. It was hosted and planned by Len Holdstock, a professor at the University of Witwatersrand. He made it possible for us to experience a very wide range of life in South Africa. I learned it is important to make it clear that you want to hear what each one has to say, including the soft-spoken and silent ones, in our experience with the group that met on the stage before an audience of 1600 in the Great Hall of the University of Witwatersrand, Johannesburg, South Africa. The group consisted of two black men, two black women, four white men, and three white women plus Carl and me as facilitators. The facilitators from the beginning assured the group each person would be heard, accepted, and valued. We had already made clear the day before we did not have the expectation of resolving conflicts only to help establish lines of communication across the lines of difference. We had already engaged in an exploration of the philosophy and principles of the PCA.

In answer to an invitation for volunteers to form a small group, a mixed group gathered and sat in a semicircle facing the large group of 1600. The time limit was an hour and a half. Bright lights illuminated the stage. We were also aware that there might be informers in the room. Altogether it seemed an impossible situation for intimate interchange to develop.

The first to speak was a black man, a leader in the Soweto community who had previous experience with the PCA. His directness and his honesty immediately called forth responses from other members of the group. From then on the facilitators responded either verbally or nonverbally to each speaker. Our verbal responses were brief, only an acknowledgement of the speaker's concern or intense feeling or an attempt at clarification. Members of the group said later that the way the facilitators helped most was the accuracy and intensity of their listening. We were also attuned to the small voices and the silent ones and several times created an opening for them to be heard. I noticed a young black man leaning forward in his seat as if ready to speak. I acknowledged him. He responded, 'This is the first time I ever spoke to a white person except to say "Yes, boss."' The interchange became deeper, personal, and more lively as time went on. There were sharp confrontations and touching moments of reconciliation.

Immediately afterward the audience was invited to express their observations and comments. At the end of the session members of the large group flooded onto the stage and became involved in animated discussion between the members of the group and themselves. Some of the recorded comments were:

'I wouldn't have believed it was possible.'

'I know now that it is possible because I have seen it happen.'
'If it's happened once, it can happen again.'
'We've seen a man and a woman work together without competition' (A quotation paralleled in the Soviet Union).
'Everybody who partook of that group was changed' (1995 comment).

I'm still not sure to whom 'everybody' referred to in that last comment. I do know that six of the members of that small group have become very active in applying the principles of the PCA in their communities and their professions and continue to do so as of 1998. We found a hunger for deep communication, for clear and real communication based on caring, wherever we went in South Africa.

It is important that someone provide the facilitative conditions – Moscow 1986

Concerning facilitators, what matters is that someone provides the facilitative conditions, whether it is designated facilitators or facilitative members of the group. In groups in which most of the participants are experienced in the PCA, facilitative members of the group are sufficient. In groups large or small in which most of the participants do not have a background in the PCA, facilitators are important, even necessary, if a growthful climate is to be provided. By growthful climate I mean one in which the individual is permitted to make his/her own choices without being controlled by the power or 'expertise' of other members of the group. I refer back to our experience mentioned earlier on the stage in Johannesburg in 1982. I believe that growth for individuals in the group in a brief time span would not have taken place without the presence of experienced facilitators. I also cite our work with a group of approximately 40–45 in Moscow. The expectation with which I entered the group was that in a repressed society such as theirs, persons would be hesitant to speak or would be very controlled in their first attempts. Not so! The first day began with a long controversy over who should be included and who should not be included. There were charges and countercharges. Anger flared and mounted to vituperation. Carl and I were attacked with, 'Why aren't you doing anything? You have done nothing! This could go on all weekend. We'll be nowhere.' We were accused of conspiring to stir up controversy in order to stimulate reaction. I still remember clearly, and this memory is supported by a journal kept at the time, that my main intervention was to hold up both hands to attract attention and then to say, 'When several people are talking at once, I can hear no one and I want to hear what each of you has to say.' There would be a pause, the tension briefly reduced, then again the mounting storm. Carl and I agreed during a break that at the end of the day we would address the group with a suggestion that we all sit in silence for five minutes before leaving the room and that we leave in silence. When we convened the next morning there was a slower pace and more listening. The accusations became more personal and were directed to individuals, e.g. 'I've always hated you with your nicey-nice ways, but I've never dared to tell you. Yesterday I got to say it.' Often there followed a brief interchange person to person.

Our interventions continued as assurances that we wanted to hear everyone, that we wanted to understand, that we cared about each person there. Carl suggested we break into triads, which he called empathy labs, for three quarters of an hour. Triads consisted of a client, a therapist, and an observer. At the end of 15 minutes they switched positions until each member had sat in the seat of the therapist, the client, and the observer. Every member of the group became involved in this activity, including those who had been silent.

Political comments were avoided but by the fourth day many members of the group, frequently referring to their experience in the triads, were sharing deeply their painful experiences with their marriages, their parents, their children, and their colleagues.

A week later Alexey Matushkin, the director of the Institute for Pedagogical Psychology, invited Carl and me to report to the Scientific Council of the Academy on the effects of the intensive weekend group. We declined in favor of asking participants to make their own reports. It seemed significant that he called alternatively a man and a woman among those who volunteered to speak. Time did not permit hearing the more than 30 volunteers. But the following three quotations are representative.

The first speaker was a man, a university professor who had thought the PCA was alright for the West but it wouldn't work for him. 'Now I know we can do it ourselves.'

The second speaker was a woman, a social worker:

> I have such strong reactions. I have been longing to share something. Yesterday I began my work with clients and I found I was starting to apply this approach. It was very important to me as a professional. I have learned that clients or friends don't want your advice, your interpretation. Before the workshop I was kind of a detective, trying to investigate, to find the underlying reason for this or that act. But then in the workshop I was the client and I learned it was very bad to be listened to by a detective. I hadn't really listened. I realized it meant a lot just to be listened to. I don't want to find some theoretical model. I just want to listen, to give my attention. I know this sounds commonplace, but I want you to realize what I've been feeling. I shouldn't treat others as objects on which we are going to try to impose our help. Formerly, I based my work on the idea that a person coming to me for help was guilty of something. When they feel guilty and we reinforce that guilt, it does not help.
>
> Working with a person yesterday, I tried to understand her pain, feeling her feelings. This was very helpful. She told me of beating her child. Formerly I would have been indignant, but this time I listened and understood. When she left she told me that it was the first time in her life that she felt understood. I have learned that it is important to stand in the other person's shoes. Before this I knew the theories. Now we have learned from the inside.

Here again there was a crying hunger for communication and self-empowerment. After the social worker, a man said, 'This process was moving without a motor. Nobody had to lead it or guide it. It was a self-evolving process. It was like the Chekov story where they were expectantly awaiting the piano-player and the piano started playing itself.'

Carl and I trusted if we gave the group an opportunity, they would find their own way.

Deep understanding of the PCA on the part of the facilitators is important – Witwatersrand 1986

There are a number of points that can be made about the intensive group at the University of Witwatersrand in Johannesburg, South Africa in 1986. This was our second visit to South Africa. It also illustrated differences in perception about what was happening. The organization lent itself to illustrating differences in outcome after some understanding of the PCA. There were sharper conflicts and deeper responses in South Africa. This was one of the most complex and perhaps the most powerful of the workshops we facilitated. Carl also remarked in the journals of our 1986 visit to South Africa, 'This has been one of the most powerful groups in which I have ever been involved'.

I think this workshop has had far-reaching effects, the most far-reaching of any of the workshops in which I have had a part. Witness that the 7th International Forum in the PCA was held in Johannesburg in 1998.

About 40 participants had been chosen. The meeting had been carefully planned by a coordinating group convened by Shirley Shochot who had a long-time acquaintance with Carl Rogers and the PCA. Carl and I were the invited facilitators. The training (I prefer the phrase 'development of facilitative skills' to 'training') plan was to meet for a long weekend (four days). Then we returned for the next weekend and gave the participants (of the previous weekend) the opportunity to split into pairs, each of which would facilitate a small group, drawn from a large meeting of 360 people. The planning group had invited residents of the area who were interested in hearing Carl speak to meet mid-week after the first weekend in a large lecture hall in another part of the campus. Then Carl and I met with 360 local residents for a half-day to discuss the PCA. It was this large group which was invited back the following weekend. The large meeting was broken into 18 small groups. Each of these groups was facilitated to the extent that it was possible by one man and one woman, one black or of colour and one white, drawn from the learners of the first weekend. Unfortunately I am not aware of other occasions on which this plan has been applied. Therein lies another challenge for the future.

It was a varied group, including a government official, a member of the African National Congress, an executive from Coca-Cola, a social worker who consulted to the medical profession and at least five participants from the small group of 11 on-stage at the '82 meeting at the same university. It was well balanced between black and white and included one or two of Indian descent.

The get-acquainted period during the first session was quite short. The group soon turned to meaningful interchange. Gradually, sharper differences began to surface. A black woman revealed that her friends and neighbors looked on her as a traitor because she was meeting with white people. She did not know if she would go home to find her family attacked or her home in flames. Both Carl and I were moved to tears. I remember that Carl moved across the circle to sit on the floor near her. I told her I did not know how I would live through such danger to myself and people I love. I could only try to imagine myself in her place.

The expressions of feeling became more intense until on the fourth day a white woman said, 'I'm ashamed of this because my black servant and her friends have been very kind to me, but when I go out on the street I sometimes wish that all the blacks would go away. They cause so much trouble.' A black woman sitting next to her shot back 'That means you wish that I would go away.'

The Coca-Cola executive told of the black servant to whom they entrusted their house and children for years but he did not know her name. He added, 'I'm ashamed of this but it's true.'

Feelings ran high. Some threatened to leave. One stood up and said, 'It's worse than I thought. I can't stand this,' and left the room. The woman from Soweto did leave the room but was brought back with the help of a white professor from the university. Several left the room but returned later. At the end of the day we announced the plan for the following weekend, wondering how many would return. There were expressions of despair and hope. While Carl expressed concern about the outcome of the workshop saying 'Maybe it won't work this time,' I was one of those who found hope in the bare honesty that permeated that day, that made evident a deep feeling of trust that they could be themselves and still be accepted.

With the exception of two or three, everyone returned the following weekend for an opportunity to practice their facilitative skills. At our closing session on the last weekend the general consensus was that 'We are a long way from settling all our differences but we have found we *can* work together'.

This workshop pointed out the value of having time to communicate experientially and having the opportunity to practice facilitative skills. This was more effective in Johannesburg than in Cape Town where the convener, a staff member and many of the participants, had little or no acquaintance with the PCA.

In 1988 I returned to Moscow with Fran Macey. My purpose was to meet with those who had been turned away in 1986 for lack of room. We met for a long weekend with a group of comparative newcomers to the PCA. At the request of Alexey Matushkin we dealt with certain questions which he had in mind about PCA, education, creativity, theory and practice of the PCA, so it was dealing mainly with technical and factual matters. During that weekend very little community spirit developed. On the last day of the workshop we submitted a questionnaire to the participants. The essence of their replies was:

- *Most helpful* was the way in which the facilitators listened deeply and let the participants know that they had understood.
- *Least helpful* was advice giving and problem solving by members of the group.

Envisaged next steps

When Carl and I left the Soviet Union and South Africa in 1986, we had already laid plans preliminary to our return the following year to meet with officials of the government and members of the diplomatic service. Chuck Devonshire and I had also made similar preliminary arrangements following a workshop in Greece in 1987. Our contacts in these three places were a step toward the implementation of the principles of the PCA at the diplomatic level. Our plans fell short when Carl died on February 4, 1987. A change of government in Greece prevented the carrying out of our hopes there.

Herein lies an unexplored challenge as we look to the future. Very few have shown either the interest, the talent, or found the opportunity to develop ways of entering the political arena on a local, national or international level. Among those few in the PCA are John Vasconcellos in California, a client and friend of Carl Rogers, who has spent more than 30 years in the State Assembly and who has been very influential. He headed the Budget Team for many years and his Task Force on Self Esteem has been noted far outside the state. Mariano Araiza-Zayas in Mexico City has a long experience of politics. His friend and colleague, Professor Alberto Segrera at the Universidad IberoAmericana is active in the local labor union. A young man in Germany, Harold Gassner, both musician and licensed psychotherapist, has been influenced by experience in several PCA workshops and is hoping to use his skills in United Nations peacekeeping. Our last word is that the people he spoke with at the UN in New York held out high hopes for his making contacts with colleagues at the UN in Bonn for the carrying out of such an enterprise. We have one member of our Experiencing Diversity (these workshops will be treated more fully in another chapter) staff , who has entered with considerable success into the politics of her local area in the state of Connecticut. These few references point to an encouraging fact: there are individuals in the world who offer the hope of realizing what now seems like a dream. Perhaps there are many others unknown to us. Still others may find encouragement to carry further their own interest or activities in this wide, unexplored field – local, national, or international politics and the PCA.

In Carl's words is it possible that this is '. . . an idea whose time has come'? Are we ready and willing to face the challenge? I cite Cecil Bodibe's quotation from Shakespeare when he invited the International Forum in the PCA to South Africa in 1998, 'There is a tide in the affairs of men which, taken at the flood, leads on to fortune.' This Forum, the 7th International Forum, was considered by a number of participants to have been the best Forum yet. Following the PCA principle that the participant is the authority on her/his experience, let me quote from one of them:

> The most impressive aspect [of the 7th International Forum] to me
> was the constructive aspect, the 'walking the talk' side. Letter(s)
> from all the Community are being sent to South African minister(s)
> [in Nelson Mandela's administration], emphasizing what the PCA
> can do, e.g. healing the wounds opened after the new revelations of

the Truth and Reconciliation Commission, initiating or sustaining dialogue between conflicting groups, for example, tribes. A magnificent donation was made to start or revive a PCA Center in South Africa. South African papers are being collected to add to Carl's and Ruth's journals of their '82 and '86 workshops and Ruth's accounts of her '87 and '95 workshops. It is hoped that the ensemble will be published as a book *The Person-Centered Approach in South Africa*. I hope the Forum papers will be published and bound or electronically published and will ask the planning committee about this. Maybe a *Forum Reader*? It's hoped to set up a task force to propose a PCA Non Governmental Organization under the UN. I hope that yet other actions will come out of the Forum.

Current developments at the highest political levels indicate that South Africa may lead the way in politics and education. In Carl's words, 'Do we dare?'

References
Kirschenbaum, H. (1979) *On Becoming Carl Rogers*, New York: Delacorte.
Rogers, C.R. (1970) *On Encounter Groups*, New York: Harper and Row.
Rogers, C.R. (1977) *On Personal Power,* New York: Delacorte.
Rogers, C.R. (1980) *A Way of Being*, Boston: Houghton Mifflin.

PCA Groups: Past, Present . . . and Future?

2

Mhairi MacMillan and Colin Lago

What has gone on over the last twenty years in person-centred approach groups? We cannot give a complete answer to this question but, in this chapter, we describe some elements of recent group activity (particularly in Britain and Europe) and some of the factors that have shaped and influenced it. We consider, for example, whether the large group or its pseudonymous counterpart the 'community meeting' has been sidetracked (or even hi-jacked) by the huge growth in counsellor training programmes, and, whether, counsellor training apart, there is a case for the continuation of group workshops, and what might be their purpose, use or direction.

Some workshops ran annually for a number of years – the Cross-Cultural Communication workshops claimed a twenty-two-year history, the FDI Britain workshops lasted eight years under the first staff team and eleven years with the second. Both sets of workshops (which shared common beginnings in the work of Charles Devonshire and his colleagues) have now ceased. On the other hand, some innovative and influential workshops were one-off events, which either could not be repeated or were simply unique for their time and place.

Large group workshops and other programmes
FDI (Facilitator Development Institute) workshops
In 1975 the first Facilitator Development Institute workshop was held in Glasgow, Scotland. Its purpose was stated as giving 'experience and theory in the facilitation of groups' (FDI brochure). About the same time, FDI workshops were being convened in Holland, Germany and France. The times were right for these enterprises, 'encounter' was in vogue, and innovation was still possible in such fields as education, social work and counselling, then still in its infancy. In 1978 Carl Rogers visited Britain for the first time. He attended part of the FDI workshop and co-convened a large group workshop in Nottingham. The excitement and sense of freedom that were experienced by many participants only partly illustrates the seminal influence of these workshops in introducing the person-centred approach

and the work of Carl Rogers to participants who came both from Britain and abroad and from a wide range of professions. But, as described elsewhere (Barkham, ch 8 below) the FDI co-directors left the workshops and moved on to other things – counsellor training and other learning programmes with an associated annual international large group meeting.

The Zinal workshop
Freshness and innovation were hallmarks of the 1981 Zinal workshop. Organised by a team of Swiss adherents of the person-centred approach (including veterans of the La Jolla programme), calling themselves 'the Swiss Group', and lasting ten days, this unique event broke new ground by eschewing 'staff/participant distinctions'. The Swiss Group wrote: 'Here, all are invited as equal participants. All may contribute, all may facilitate. There will be no designated staff, no "superstars"'. At the start, many people still imagined facilitation to be the responsibility of the conveners, who had consistently to make their position clear. Some participants attributed the chaotic and frustrating beginning of the workshop to be due to the lack of facilitators. As time went on, the issue was forgotten, no longer of importance because virtually everyone was involved. There were certainly a number of people known to have 'facilitative skills' but it seemed that, for them, it was a definite relief and a great sense of freedom not to be in the role of facilitator.

Neither did the workshop have official translators. The conveners had simply stated: 'The workshop will take place in English, French and German. We hope you can speak at least one of these three languages'. Various developments followed. People wanted to speak their own national tongue and to hear those of others. Different languages were heard. Translations became the responsibility of the whole group. At first, a few able linguists carried the load; then more and more people started to use languages they barely knew and even to translate for others who knew even less of a particular language than they did. Had there been 'official' translators, it is likely that participants would have refrained from trying out their own latent language skills and put the responsibility on to the translators. This is what has happened in workshops, such as the Cross-Cultural Communication workshops where official translation was set up. It is a fine illustration of conveners not doing for the group what it can do for itself (Wood, ch 9, this volume). The group finds out what it can do only through necessity.

Istanbul 1998 (La Jolla Program International)
Another one-off workshop was convened in 1988 in Istanbul, Turkey, under the aegis of the La Jolla Program International. The large group was composed of about 140 people, of whom over 100 were Turkish. There were a few participants from India, the rest European or American. This was a rare experience of a workshop taking place within a culture different from the western European–North American one. It is profoundly affecting to hear the ezan (call to prayer) early in the morning and throughout the day, and to see all around a skyline punctuated by minarets. English had been designated as the working language, but the large

number of Turkish participants, and the refusal of some of them to accept this kind of 'English language imperialism' resulted in the widespread use of Turkish (and other languages). The issue was carried over to at least one small group (numbering twenty-five) and brought out the deeply felt need for a person's right to use their own language be acknowledged and for the whole group to take responsibility for understanding each other.

Three other forms of large group meeting
During the 80s and 90s, three forms of international large group meeting came into existence. The first workshop in the series 'Person-Centered Approach to Cross-Cultural Communication' took place in 1981 in Mannheim, Germany and was instigated by Charles Devonshire. Participants formed teams from individual countries, organised by a country coordinator. They were also associated with a number of learning programmes taking place in different countries in Europe. These workshops have been written about elsewhere (see, for example, McIlduff and Coghlan, 1989; MacMillan and Lago, 1993, 1996). The Cross-Cultural Workshops have now ceased.

Oaxtepec, Mexico was the location for the first International Forum on the Person-Centered Approach, convened by Alberto Segrera in 1982. Initially people attended by invitation. This format did not persist. Perhaps it was seen as being antagonistic to a supposedly person-centred value of autonomous choice; perhaps it was a practical development as past-participant lists grew longer and the existence of the Forums became more common knowledge in the burgeoning international PCA community. In any case, each Forum was coloured according to the country and the national organising group: Mexican, British, American, Brazilian, Dutch, Greek and South African. At La Jolla, USA, in 1987, the third Forum was, in part, a memorial to Carl Rogers who had died a few months previously. Naturally, many people grieved and no doubt all missed his presence.

The forums included presentations of papers and topic workshops as well as optional small group meetings and 'community' meetings. They focused on the Person-centred Approach in its wider applications rather than being confined to therapy. The forums continue, with the next scheduled for the year 2001 in Japan.

Thirdly, in 1988 Germain Lietaer founded the International Conference on Client-Centered and Experiential Psychotherapy (ICCCEP) in Leuven, Belgium. These conferences were intended to embody a scholarly and scientific reporting of developments in the areas of theory, research and practice. At the conferences, the explicit 'group' element was minimal. There were no community meetings scheduled. At the second ICCCEP, small discussion and support groups were timetabled, but the emphasis remains on the 'scientific' aspects of client- (or person-) centred therapy. The conferences also continue, with the next planned for the year 2000 in Chicago.

A question might be asked here: do certain people attend ICCCEP conferences, while others participate in International Forums, and still others take part in large group workshops? The answer seems to be that there is indeed some separation.

Conferences, for example, are attended by some professional therapists and researchers who might not go to a Forum (not now, at any rate, since part of their function has been taken over by the conferences). The Forums have been attended by persons active in the person-centred approach, not necessarily therapists. Large group workshops are participated in by those interested in 'the phenomenon of group'. There is much overlap amongst these categories.

Impact of counsellor training on large groups
The last ten years (from 1988–98) have seen a huge increase in counselling and counselling training courses. An ever increasing number of participants in large group workshops were found to be working in counselling, as counsellors, counsellor trainers or trainees. Many, if not all training courses in the person-centred approach to counselling and psychotherapy use the group as a learning community within the training course context. The so-called 'large group' or 'community meeting' (Mearns, 1997 (a) and (b); Fairhurst and Merry, ch 3 below) occupies a valued place, but is likely to be much smaller than a large group in the workshop context. Indeed, 'small groups' in many workshops have been larger than 'large groups' on counselling training courses.

Regarding the 'personality factors' of counsellors, trainers and trainees, Mearns (1997b) has said that they 'favour disorder in the neurotic direction'. What he means by this is 'a tendency towards taking excessive responsibility, being emotionally over-responsive and prone to guilt'. If this is valid, we can imagine what the effect on large group process might be. For one thing, there is likely to be a tendency towards less risk-taking, less willingness to be seen as 'deviant' and more reliance on unmitigated empathic responding. It is no longer so 'risky' to speak of one's personal pain or trauma – for there is almost certain to be an empathic response, but it may be very risky to 'come out' as being (perhaps) fed up with the relating of personal wounds (especially when the same story is told in group after group) and with the tyranny of 'just expressing my feelings'. It has been speculated that the prevailing therapy culture may foster the spread of 'woundology', that is, defining ourselves by our wounds and consequently needing to be with 'people who speak the same language and share the same mind-set and behaviours' (Myss, 1997: 6). Arguably, a tendency for some participants in large groups to seek this shared culture of woundology may be growing. Large group workshops are not 'group therapy' as such, but perhaps it would be fair to say that empathic responding has come to have precedence over congruent relating. When one of the core conditions comes to be over-valued the operational unity of the three is disrupted.

The following points illustrate some differences between a training course community meeting and a large group convened in a workshop context.

Intention
The members of a course community meeting, first and foremost, want to be counsellors (Mearns, 1997a). They have a different investment in the group. It is not so much an investment or commitment to the success of the group *per se*, but

rather an investment in using the group as a medium in which to further their training as a counsellor. A convened large group need only have (perhaps should only have?) 'the conscious intention of coming together as a group' (Wood, ch 9 below).

Time commitment: residential or non-residential
The time that is allocated to and actually spent in the large community meeting group depends to an extent on whether the course is residential or not. The time given to community meetings on one full-time course (non-residential) is probably no more than four hours in total per week (Mearns 1997a: 153–4) and is less for a part-time course. On a residential course, time spent in large group is almost certain to be much longer, perhaps an average of three hours per day over a ten-day residential period. However, at a workshop, it is not unusual for the large group to meet for six or more hours in a day. Participants may come and go during that time without this being judged as detrimental to their 'training'.

Number of participants
Although the number of participants that constitutes a large group varies greatly, on most training courses the 'large group' – whose number may be from fifteen to twenty-four (Fairhurst and Merry, ch 3 below), or from twenty to forty people (Mearns, 1997a: 153) or, on training courses that we have been associated with, from ten to eighteen – would be considered a 'small group' at a large group workshop. People coming off training courses, whose experiences of a 'large group' has been confined to the 'community meeting' of the training course, often, understandably, present the same behaviour in a large group of fifty to three hundred people and try to make the same kind of responses.

Structure and role of facilitators/trainers
Another essential difference concerns the time structuring and agenda setting of the group and the roles played in it by the 'staff'. On group workshops the degree of pre-set structure is usually minimal. The group conveners may do only 'that which the group cannot do for itself' (Wood, ch 9 below): find a suitable location, sending out invitations or advertising, set a start and finish time, and so on. The 'community meeting' of a large group workshop, therefore, is the agency for conceiving and building the structure of the workshop. On at least one clutch of counselling training courses, the 'community meeting' may be the agency for changing the already tightly-knit structure of the course (Mearns, 1997a). But, to make changes to an existing structure is much less 'free' than the freedom to not only make, but also to continually modify, the structure as the workshop proceeds. Some training courses, or 'learning programmes' allow the group more power (and responsibility) for determining the programme (see, for example, Fairhurst and Merry, ch 3 below).

The phenomenon of parallel processing emerges in the relationship between what happens in the staff group and what happens in the large group (MacMillan and Lago, 1993). In other words, 'the group process mirrors the staff process' (Mearns, 1997a: 164). The effect is more damaging the more any struggles within the staff group are unexpressed in the large group meeting. When the 'staff' are also 'trainers' their roles and responsibilities differ from 'conveners' of a large group workshop. One important difference is that on a training course, there must be a method of assessment, no matter how student-centred or 'individually assessed' it is, and trainers are involved in that assessment process. The relationships and dynamics between training course staff will be quite different from those between conveners of a large group. Not that it will necessarily be easier with the latter. At the Sedona large group in 1998, the conveners had some sharp issues with each other; but these were brought into the large group meeting and dealt with openly.

Much has been made of the way in which experience in training course groups (large and small) can provide some of the same gains that accrue from personal therapy and more besides (Mearns, 1997a, ch 7). But paradoxically, when the group is embedded in the context of a training course, it is less able to fulfil freely (unconditionally) its potential to become a forum for expression of experiencing and for real negotiation of meaning.

Theoretical principles underlying the person-centred approach in groups
As long as the person-centred approach in groups was seen as a development of client-centred therapy, it was taken as sufficient theoretical explanation that the same principles applied as in the clinical setting of the counselling process (see, for example, Rogers, 1970, 1987; Thorne, 1988). There are differing views on the transferability of experience as a therapist into the role of group facilitator. Thorne (1988: 202) believes that the skills required of a large group facilitator are 'unlikely to be attained by someone who is not deeply involved in therapeutic work in the course of his or her professional life'. This is because of the 'level and intensity of empathic listening and communicating which is required'. In contrast, Beck (1974: 456) questions whether a leader whose previous training has been in individual therapy may be able to hold a group-wide perspective, and speculates that s/he may 'feel overwhelmed by his concern for attending to several clients simultaneously'. When does a therapeutic orientation (both of designated facilitators, if any, and of participants) and the 'skills' of empathic listening and responding, in fact hold back the development of the group's transpersonality – its 'we-intentionality'?

It has become increasingly obvious that seeing the large group only as a theatre for the enactment of the three 'core conditions' (congruence, empathic understanding, and unconditional positive regard) fails to capture the complexity inherent in it. Such an 'application' view might just be capable of explaining small group process but helps very little when it comes to large groups (see Wood ch 9, Coulson, ch 10 below). Not only does complexity increase when groups are larger, but also because of the increasing sophistication of participants as more and more of them attend group after group. We can refer to theories from science to help us gain some understanding of what might be going on in the dynamics of the large group. The Theory of Formative Causation about 'the build-up of habits in nature through the process of morphic resonance' (Sheldrake, 1995: x) which, in positing the presence of the past', suggests how earlier group experiences may affect later ones. Some other theoretical developments may also have a bearing on the large group such as chaos theory (Gleick, 1987; Sanford, unpublished) and complexity theory. The last suggests that development occurs at the edge of chaos and order, neither fully in one or the other condition. Perhaps 'PCA work with . . . groups is also possible only at the edge of chaos and order' (Hlavenka, 1995).

Some theoretical statements
Carl Rogers (1970, 1977, 1980) reiterated his belief that there were many different modes of being facilitative. He stressed that his way was just that, his way, and he did not expect others to imitate him, nor did he act as a model for anyone. All the same, Rogers disliked those leaders who relish 'dramatics' in a group, evaluating it according to how many have wept or have become enraptured. And he saw trust destroyed by those who manipulate the group towards some unspoken goal of their own. Nor did he approve of a 'one-note song' type of facilitation, where only one mode was considered valid.

He made it clear that he was distinguishing between behaviour which would be acceptable for a participant in the group, but not for the labelled facilitator. The reason for this distinction is that he believed a facilitator's behaviour 'tends to set a norm for the group' whereas corresponding behaviour from a participant 'will be very adequately handled by the group members themselves'. In the case of a group with 'conveners' but not 'facilitators', it may be that this behaviour would not be so much of a problem.

More pervasive, perhaps, is when group interactions lack openness and honesty. Bebout (1974) confirms this view by referring to 'group incongruence or deceit' as a perhaps decisive factor in leading a group to fail. This is most difficult to overcome when the incongruence or self-deceit is perpetuated by the staff members. This is likely to make the development of 'experiential communality' impossible.

Empathy – experiential communality
The experience of empathy within groups goes further (and deeper) than empathic, reflective responding (cf Wood, ch 9 this volume). An (apparently) simple empathic response may have its place, but cannot be churned out routinely. Groups have become more sophisticated than this. In a similar way, in a therapy context, clients are often more informed about the person-centred approach – many have undertaken some level of counselling training – and can spot 'reflecting back' a mile away. They may even point this out to their therapists. Yet empathic processes are still essential to the building of 'experiential communality' (Bebout, 1974). A feature of empathic processing in groups – especially large groups – is likely to be 'idiosyncratic empathy' (Bozarth, 1984). In therapy, Bebout suggests, empathy is most often of a 'vicarious' mode; that is, it has an 'as if' feeling. But other modes of empathy are also possible, which come to the fore to a greater extent in the

group context. These include physiognomic empathy (connecting with the bodily 'felt sense' of another) and cognitive empathy (assimilation of others' values, meanings, symbols, intentions and ideation).

Experiential communality is described as 'the simultaneous sharing of emotional experience' and, perhaps, personal meaning. 'Both a physical state of arousal (felt sensation) and a self-meaning context must be isomorphic to arrive at experiential communality' (Bebout, 1974: 377).

Bebout was writing of the phenomenon in respect of encounter groups. When we come to look at large group processes, experiential communality takes on a wider dimension. Another sense of experiential communality is a feeling like 'We're all in this together'. Bebout gives the example of the closeness between those few workers who have struggled through a snowstorm to make it into the office. Bebout suggests that a quality of experiential communality is that it 'can by itself evoke an expanded sense of self' (Bebout, 1974: 379). It may be that experiential communality is a forerunner of the experience of 'unity' in large groups referred to by Coulson (ch 10) and Wood (ch 9) in this volume.

Large group seminars, 1996

At the 1995 Forum in Greece, Lago and MacMillan made a presentation on the Large Group, with the title: Large Groups – Dodging the issue? This title was partly inspired by two articles from the journal *Counselling*. In his article The Need for Connectedness and Community in a Masturbatory Society a critique of individual therapy and the cultural bias towards it, Lago (1994) suggests:

> . . . our cultural beliefs in individualism, intensified in recent decades by political and economic forces, have had alienating effects upon our society. The pathology which we as counsellors can so easily see in individuals is also manifest in society. Group work in general and large groups in particular, offer a forum in which these complex issues of relatedness, the management of power, decision making and active democracy can be explored by participants.

But what if these large groups continue, in their concentration on individual feelings especially past emotional trauma, to perpetuate that same cult of the individual? One way that this is fostered is by the continuation of the 'counselling' type of response that is learned in training school, and modelled, consciously or unconsciously both by trainees and by some long-time practising counsellors and therapists. May this not obscure for us the growth and development of the experiencing of the group itself?

The second article, Mentoring as Change Agency (O'Brien, 1995), highlighted the possibility of the group becoming 'locked into process at the expense of task' and commented: 'The group may enjoy being together and may be strongly creative, but produce little of value to the organisation as a whole and may become increasingly marginalised'. The question was asked, 'What might we consider to be the task of large groups, in the context of the person-centred approach, which is (as has been pointed out, Wood, ch 9 below) not an organisation, but merely an approach?'

The presentation invited the group to consider this question and to generate ideas and further questions about research into large groups. A sizable number participated in this session and most enthusiastically contributed a wide range of ideas and concerns. These clustered around specific themes as listed below.

Technical aspects of large groups
- What building and room designs contribute best to such workshops?
- Are microphones necessary? (Groups of 200–300 were regular occurrences in Europe and the United States; even larger in Brazilian workshops).
- What impact do microphones have on the group?
- Is the provision of translators helpful, even necessary, or inappropriate and disabling?
- How is any translation process set up and should translators have their own support group?

Ideas related to research methodology
- Would it be possible to agree on one written statement from the whole group, however short?
- Can the common denominators of participants' experiencing be understood and recorded?
- The complexity of the large group and the challenge it poses to the research process.
- Consistency of the research model with the phenomenon of the large group was considered as vital.
- A phenomenological methodology that attempted to describe the process as it occurred was proposed.
- Research to be framed in such a way that we do not confirm what we hypothesise, we need to search for what we do not understand. Previous research must not be ignored.
- Any research needs to incorporate the whole event, not just the group sessions (e.g. to include social time events).

An understanding of meaning
- Attempts to collate the range of meaning in the group.
- What happens in the silence, between the words?
- Explore alternatives to spoken language.

Exploration of emotional life
- Why are 'expectation' and 'fear' two commonly used words in the large group?
- Elicit and name the fears and expectations of what 'we' want to happen, what 'we' are afraid might happen.

- Physiological arousal related to emotional expression is frequently reported.

The challenge of creating the core conditions
- Can a way be found to accept and respect all the participants in the group?
- Can we learn to live with more understanding with more people?
- The importance of an opening ritual.
- The establishment of social inclusion and the analysis of exclusionary factors.

Other points addressed
- Purpose: is there a larger purpose in studying this phenomenon?
- Perception: recognition of the multiple levels of perceptual reality.
- Follow-up studies required: what happens to participants afterwards – are they in some way different?
- The need to continue to explore facilitative behaviour.
- Impotence in the large group: when participants feel they cannot speak, move, relate, etc.
- How does the culture of a group form?
- What can and cannot (easily) be spoken of in the large group? why?
- Parallel experiencing: when a small group away from the large group discusses an issue and returns to find the large group raising the same issue. How might this happen?
- Does the large group cause a ripple effect afterwards?
- In its often chaotic process the large group has enormous potential to stimulate concerns and questions – but is the small group more productive in locating solutions?
- Power relations: how is power created, used and shared? How is power wielded by the organisers, the facilitator group, etc?

The following summer, 1996, we (the editors) organised three seminars on The Large Group which took place in different parts of Britain (the Norwich Centre, Moray House Institute of Education, Edinburgh and the University of Sheffield). They were advertised through person-centred networks and conference mailing lists. The purpose of the seminars was described as 'to bring together people experienced in large groups of whatever tradition (e.g. person-centred, group analytic, community-building) and to engage in considering the task of researching large groups'. It was preferred that participants would have had experience of a large group. We had applied for and were granted partial funding by the British Academy, in the form of a Visiting Professorship to John K. Wood, thus enabling him and Lucila Machado Assumpcao to come from Brazil.

The format for each seminar day included an introduction to the project team followed by an expanded outline of the purpose of the seminar. John K. Wood then gave a short presentation of some of the issues worthy of consideration for research. A short paper written by John Wood on studying large groups, was available to participants and Lucila Assumpcao had prepared a piece of art work, *Construir o Uno* (based on the notion that art can make tangible what is intangible) to encourage each participant's engagement with the purpose.

A wide range of concerns, anxieties and ideas were discussed during the three days. The following are from the reflective recordings made by John Wood:

> • *The group and the individual:* is it possible to think together about our collective behaviour as well as focus attention on the subjective feelings of individuals in the group?
>
> • *What about the Hawthorne effect?* i.e. the bringing about of change by the very activity of giving someone or something attention over and above 'normal' levels. Although researchers usually try to eliminate this effect, it should rather be explored further as it is such 'non-specific factors' (the so-called 'placebo effect') which count for so much that happens in organisations, groups and individuals.
>
> • *A phenomenological approach:* 'I am impressed', John records, 'how little repetition has occurred over the seminars. Each person seems to bring a different aspect of group experience to the discussion. It occurs to me that in these seminars we are in fact doing a research, a phenomenological research. Each person is putting into words an expression of a part of the phenomenon of large group. As Goethe might say, the phenomenon is actually speaking for itself, through itself, that is, through its parts.'

Facilitation and participation
- We know that one person with the intention (conscious or unconscious) of sabotaging the sensitive deliberations of a group can do so.
- Rather than thinking that good facilitators are needed for the group to realise its potential, perhaps it requires 'good participants'.
- Some participants seemed to hold the large group process back and divert it away from the transpersonal topics that kept emerging.
- What would happen if the personal concerns expressed in encounter mode lessened and the impersonal group mind and transpersonal elements raised by some could be more fully explored?

This dimension of complexity, unitary and transpersonal, became a strong theme in the Sedona experiment, which was organised, partly, as an outcome of these seminars.

The Sedona experiment, 1998
Following these seminars, a large group was convened by Lucila Assumpcao, Peggy Natiello, and John Wood. The invitation stated:

> Our vision is a temporary community of approximately fifty persons, drawn by a common interest in large-group potential for nurturing creativity and growth. We will live and meet together for a week in

an unfolding process designed and guided only by our interactions.
Each of us will become a researcher of his/her own experience. The
more carefully we unravel the threads of our particular involvement
in this experiment, the more we will understand:
- the dynamics that transform a group from a conflicted gathering
  of individuals into a harmonious whole,
- the potential movement from individual power struggles to a
  synergetic group power,
- the ways to use self to contribute to a group culture,
- the balance between autonomy and merging,
- the transpersonal aspects of group functioning.

The assembled group met in January 1998 near Sedona, Arizona, a town that has
become known for its 'vortices' or centres of electromagnetic energy in the earth's
crust. Historically, the area has been the home of several Native American tribes
including the Navaho, who believe they embody spirituality for all humans.

The location for the meeting was a conference centre, ten miles' drive on dirt
roads from the highway and seventeen miles from the town. On the day of arrival
a huge rainstorm sat over the desert and began to reduce the red clay roads to
quagmires of mud. Local residents expressed concern that if the rains continued,
the gullies would become impassable with raging flood water. The organisers were
anxious for participants travelling to the centre in hired cars and minibuses. Four-
wheel drive vehicles came out from the centre and, despite many adventures, all
arrived safely. What a start to a large group!

Preparation for this group had been extensive. All intending participants were
circulated with personal thoughts from the organisers, the paper *On Studying Large
Group Workshops* (as prepared for the seminars) and an invitation from Lucila
Assumpcao to consider their experiencing at different stages in the journey towards
Sedona. At least one participant was angry to receive some of this, believing, it
seemed, that she felt it as some kind of pressure on her to do something.

Any extensive reflecting on the Sedona experiment needs to include
contributions from many of those present. Maureen O'Hara undertook to develop
the research aspect and the result of this is awaited. The following is a reaction
from one of the editors:

> Some eight months after the Sedona workshop ended, it seems to
> me now that the greatest significance was that it took place at all.
> Sixty people from all over the United States and Europe gathered
> together in a remote place in the Arizona desert. If it were the case
> that I had 'had to go', it was in a sense also true that everyone else
> 'had' to be there. This is not making a claim for the 'specialness' of
> this event; what would have been (was?) special was the deliberate
> conscious choice of everyone to participate.
>
> Yet I must confess to some disappointment with the outcome. I
> believe that the 'conscious intention' to take part was somehow

squandered. One question for me is: what is the basis on which intimacy can be established? I found myself almost unmoved by personal stories of trauma, of devastating childhood or the deaths of close relatives. It may have been because I had heard some of the stories before, from the same people. I think this is a key: had these people been clients in a counselling situation, I would have accepted the necessity of telling the story over and over again. This was not a therapy situation but I seemed to find myself being put into the role of a therapist and having to be empathic and apparently unconditionally accepting. There were many therapists present, and sound, sincere therapeutic responses were made. I felt very distant and unable to say so. Perhaps my 'therapist' persona was too strong to be easily overruled.

Only briefly and towards the end of this workshop did glimpses of communal thinking and community sensing begin to peek out and these are discussed in more detail in the chapter by Alan Coulson.

The need for connectedness and community

For me it is thoughts of the climate of hot war and a hot planet that necessitate large group work. In my experience one-to-one therapy and group therapy are undertaken originally out of a feeling of necessity: few embark on and persevere with such therapy just for the interest of it. Similarly there is an urgent need to understand the rhythms of past and present cultures, and, in turn, their relation to the rhythms of the planet (Steiner, 1991).

The title of this section is derived directly from an article written several years ago (Lago, 1994). Dating from his first attendance at a large cross-cultural group in Szeged, Hungary, 1984, Colin has been profoundly interested in the possibilities of the application of such experiences to the wider social world.

The central tenets of the article are described briefly here. The late twentieth century (particularly in western countries) has seen a rise in aggressive individualism. Researchers such as Geert Hofstede (1980), on cultural differences, and John Kingdom (1992), on the sociology of individualism, have charted this tendency. The activity of counselling/psychotherapy, whilst profoundly defensible on the individual level, could be argued to be a contributor to this individualising tendency through reinforcing a withdrawal from the social, cultural and political worlds in a manner that is ultimately unhealthy for community and society – the collective (see Hillman and Ventura, 1992).

Lago acknowledges the importance of the continued drive towards professionalisation of the various therapeutic groups. However, critical questions are also posed to the profession in relation to the less recognised implications of its focus on individuals. The field of transcultural counselling, for example, has long recognised that individual pathology is directly related to societal pathology. Is it the individual or society that is sick? Kingdom (1992) has noted a breakdown in the sense of community in recent decades through changing patterns of employment and unemployment, the breakdown of extended nuclear families, the effects of poverty and so on. In short, Lago argues that therapists (amongst others) must pay attention to the creation of connectedness and community.

In a powerful statement, de Mare sums up this situation:

> If we are to survive at all we can no longer put off the day when the psychological, the politico-economic and the socio-cultural contexts must meet operationally in a unified field (de Mare, 1975).

Such a view, however, seems to have been resisted strongly by the majority of the therapeutic community – see Samuels (1993) for a report of an international survey on 'Political Material in the Clinical Setting'. Steiner notes that 'as an example of cultural defect, it is remarkable how the areas covered by psychiatry, by psychoanalysis, by psychotherapy and group therapy all avoid a critique of the cultural contexts in which they are being practised. Attempts to explore this context are treated as 'unrealistic' (Steiner, in de Mare et al, 1991: xviii). From the analytic perspective, de Mare et al (1991) note that 'a person can be as unaware of their cultural assumptions as they are of their unconscious'.

Carl Rogers certainly believed in the importance of the person-centred facilitated group in bringing about constructive social change.

> We cannot escape the conviction that a facilitative person-centred climate in a group, a climate which is known and which others can also create, is an extremely powerful influence in decreasing tensions, creating greater harmony. Increasingly, we have the conviction that most major changes are precipitated by a great stress or crisis; that a person and perhaps a nation, pushed to the brink of disaster can respond by panic and disintegration, by violence against others or themselves, or by openness to the pain and the risk of accepting change (Rogers and Sanford, 1991).

He lived out this belief in his work in Northern Ireland, South Africa and the USSR (Sanford, ch 1, this volume). Nevertheless, he acknowledged the risk to his professional reputation and to those of his colleagues who 'put their trust in very large groups and in their wisdom' (Rogers, 1980: 316). The implication is that it is safer by far to remain in the world of one-to-one psychotherapy and counselling or at least stay with small groups.

The large group process has potentially a humanising influence. It exposes participants to multiple layers of reasoning, dialogue, perception, reflection and so on as played out by the relationship dynamics and interactions of all present. Serious human matters including race, class, disability, gender, sexuality, cultural practices, politics, and power relationships are extensively discussed and a multiplicity of viewpoints pronounced. The large group can therefore be experienced as anxiety-inducing and the only strategy to deal with this may be to leave. The expression of a multiplicity of views, often made in an apparently chaotic sequence may be too much to bear for some, particularly if they are in a psychologically fragile state. The brochures distributed to advertise both the FDI workshops (Barkham, ch 8, this volume) and the series of Cross-Cultural Communication workshops in Europe from 1981–94, carried a cautionary reminder that participants were responsible for themselves, and that those currently in therapy should check out with their therapists that they were 'up to' such an experience at the time.

Groups, therefore, offer the possibility of relatedness, a sense of interconnectedness, can be humanising in their process and provide a profound learning experience. Inevitably, as creative gatherings, they may also, for some individuals induce considerable fear, anxiety and dislocation from that individual's own view of the world. At best, large group experiences facilitate an enhanced understanding of the complexities of the social and political world we all live in. To reiterate Lago's (1994) statement:

> The time is due for us as therapists, I believe, to also turn our attention
> to the needs of individuals within a societal framework.
> I am because we are (South African proverb).

What of the future?
For what may we look to large groups in the future? From the above we might imagine two possible directions, not incompatible with each other.

First, experiences in large groups (of any size) can foster awareness of a deeper, transpersonal connectedness. That is, the experience of unity in multiplicity, not by analysing the phenomenon of group but by living it. This follows on the expanded sense of 'self' and of what it means to be a person.

Second, there could be movement towards social and political action – with or without facilitation. An example 'with facilitation' is the work with Citizens' Juries (Hoffman, ch 7 below). There are two recent (January 1999) examples 'without facilitation' from the often cynically regarded political sphere. The US Senate of one hundred members met and successfully agreed on a procedure for the impeachment trial of the president. John Wood wrote to us: 'To me, there was no surprise to learn that the human potential of a large group of good-willed people, with a conscious, collective intention, having put aside conventional measures that could not apply in an unedited situation with such striking urgency, could reach a creative consensual solution' (Wood, 1999). And a smaller group, a 'cross-party consultative steering group' has just produced a co-operative, creative consensual blueprint for the operation of the coming Scottish Parliament. One group member commented, 'The best proof that this will work is the process itself' (BBC Scotland, 1999). These examples affirm an expanded sense of what human beings are capable, and of the possibilities inherent in human potential.

References

Barrett-Lennard, G.T. (1994) 'Toward a Person-Centered Theory of Community' *J of Humanistic Psychology*, 34, 3: 62–86.

Barrett-Lennard, G.T. (1998) *Carl Rogers' Helping System*. London: Sage.

BBC Scotland (1999) Reporting Scotland; 15 January.

Bennis, W. G. and Shepard, H.A. (1973) 'A Theory of Group Development' in R.T.Golembiewski and A.Blumberg (eds) *Sensitivity Training and the Laboratory Approach*, Itasca, Illinois: Peacock.

Bebout, J. (1974) It takes one to know one: Existential-Rogerian concepts in encounter groups. In D.Wexler and L.Rice,(eds) *Innovations in client-centered therapy,* New York: Wiley.

Beck, A.P. (1974) Phases in the development of structure in therapy and encounter groups. In D.Wexler and L.Rice,(eds) *Innovations in client-centered therapy,* New York: Wiley.

Bozarth, J.D. (1984) Beyond Reflection: emergent modes of empathy. In J.M.Shlien and R.Levant (eds) *Client-centered therapy and the person-centered approach,* New York: Praeger.

de Mare, P., Piper, R. and Thompson, S. *Koinonia: from hate through dialogue to culture in the large group,* London: Karnac.

de Mare, P. (1975) The Politics of Large Groups, in L.Kreeger (ed) *The Large Group: dynamics and therapy,* London: Karnac.

Gleick, J. (1987) *Chaos. Making a new science.* New York: Viking Penguin.

Hillman, J. and Ventura, M. (1992) *We've had 100 years of psychotherapy and the world's getting worse.* San Francisco: Harper.

Hlavenka, V. (1995) *Chaos, Order and PCA,* paper presented at the 5th Forum on the Person-centred Approach, Greece.

Hofstede, G. (1980) *Culture's Consequences: International differences in work related values.* Beverley Hills: Sage.

Kingdom, J. (1992) *No Such Thing as Society: individualism and community.* Buckingham: Open University Press.

Lago, C.O. (1994) 'Therapy for a Masturbatory Society: the Need for Connectedness and Community' in *Counselling*, 5, 2.

McIlduff, E. and Coghlan, D. (1989) Process and facilitation in a cross-cultural communication workshop, *Person-Centered Review*, 4,1.

MacMillan, M.I. and Lago, C.O. (1993) Large Groups: Critical Reflections and Some Concerns, *The Person-centered Approach and Cross-cultural Communication: an International Review*, vol. 2.

MacMillan, M.I. and Lago, C.O. (1996) The Facilitation of Large Groups: Participants' Experiences of Facilitative Moments, In R. Hutterer, G. Pawlowsky, P. Schmid and R. Stipsits (eds) *Client-centered and Experiential Psychotherapy: a Paradigm in Motion,* Frankfurt: Peter Lang.

Mearns, D. (1997a) *Person-centred Counsellor Training.* London: Sage.

Mearns, D. (1997b) Achieving the personal development dimension in professional counsellor training. *Counselling*, 8, 2.

Myss, C. (1997) *Why People don't Heal and How They Can.* London: Bantam.

O'Brien, J. (1995) Mentoring as change agency – a psychodynamic approach. *Counselling, 6,* 1.

Rogers, C.R. (1970) *Encounter Groups.* London: Penguin.

Rogers, C.R. (1977) *On Personal Power.* London: Constable.

Rogers, C.R. (1980) *A Way of Being.* Boston: Houghton Mifflin.

Rogers, C.R. (1987) Client-centered? Person-centered? *Person-Centered Review,* 2,1.

Rogers, C.R. and Sanford, R. (1991) Reflections on our South African Experience; *The Person-centered Approach and Cross-cultural Communication: an International Review,* vol. 2.

Samuels, A. (1993) *The Political Psyche.* London: Routledge.

Sanford, R. (unpublished) The person-centred approach and chaos: from Rogers to Gleick and back again.

Sheldrake, R. (1995) *Seven Experiments that Could Change the World..* London: Fourth Estate.

Steiner, P.P. (1991) Foreword to de Mare, P., Piper, R. and Thompson, S., *Koinonia: from hate through dialogue to culture in the large group.* London: Karnac.

Thorne, B. (1998) The Person-centred Approach to Large Groups. In M. Aveline and W. Dryden (eds) *Group Therapy in Britain.* Buckingham: Open University Press.

Wood, J. K. (1999) personal communication.

TRAINING AND DEVELOPMENT

Group Work in Client-Centred Counsellor Training

3

Irene Fairhurst and Tony Merry

Introduction

Discussion of the role of group work in the specific context of counsellor training is relatively under-represented in the literature. A recent article (Irving and Williams, 1996) reports that there is no evidence for group work as an essential component of effective training, argues that it is not clear what skills, developed through group work, can be utilised in individual counselling settings, and questions the suitability and effectiveness of groups for some individuals in training. Lyons (1997) takes the opposite view, believing, with the evidence of feedback from many group participants over five years, that effectively facilitated groups promote the development of transferable skills and attitudes.

Mearns (1994) argues for the importance of large unstructured groups in the training of person-centred counsellors, particularly with regard to the development of counsellor congruence. He makes the important point that the mere *portrayal* of empathic understanding and acceptance is difficult to sustain in a large group where such behaviour is more likely to be challenged, and as the group develops, this portrayal gives way to more congruent expressions of unconditional positive regard and empathy (p. 42).

In a later discussion, Mearns (1997a) identifies eight functions of large groups in counsellor training that include the sharing of information, communal decision making, raising both personal issues and those concerning the course, working with conflict, keeping track of realities, and 'coming out' in which individuals share part of their personal process with the group, as well as experimenting with congruence.

Charleton (1996) has discussed the training of counsellors, emphasising the role of 'self-directed learning', and has examined a number of issues concerning the part that groups play in the development of self-awareness, and the acquisition of the skills of attending, responding, disclosing, and challenging (p. 103). She sees a great deal of value in trainees experiencing a range of group work situations providing staff facilitators are able to prevent individuals from being hurt, scapegoated or stereotyped. Charleton also discusses the ways in which groups can be used to examine fundamental issues in counselling such as confidentiality, the use of language and attitudes to oppression, for example.

Brodley and Merry (1995), rather than discussing group working skills, refer, as does Mearns (1994, 1997a), more to the importance of the group in the development of the values and attitudes central to effective person-centred counselling. Brodley and Merry define the aim of person-centred peer groups as being the creation of '. . . the facilitative climate of Rogers' therapeutic attitudes in the group. The therapeutic climate promotes individual and group goals by facilitating constructive relationships among participants and open sharing of experiences and ideas so they can learn from each other' (p. 17).

Raskin, in his two-part review of client-centred group psychotherapy (Raskin, 1986a, 1986b), identifies the recurring theme that person-centred group work in any context is underpinned by the same set of values and attitudes as is individual psychotherapy. Trust in each person's capacity for self-determination and the belief that individuals have within themselves the necessary resources for self-development are, of course, defining features of person-centred psychology generally. In the various contexts described by Raskin, common features include the manifestation in the group of expressions of empathic understanding, a desire for authentic and congruent communication, and a consistently high level of non-judgemental respect for individuals. The leader's or 'facilitator's' role remains essentially non-directive (there are few, if any, games, or structured exercises described in the person-centred literature), and the emphasis is on the facilitator as a participating, real and spontaneous person.

A comprehensive account of the history of small and large groups in various situations, including cross-cultural communication work and conflict exploration, for example, is given in Barrett-Lennard (1998). Whilst Barrett-Lennard describes how person-centred groups have led to significant learning for many of their participants, little is included on the impact of such groups specifically in counsellor training programmes, reflecting the paucity of the literature on groups in this context.

In counsellor training courses, the staff facilitator's role is complicated by the fact that staff members also have other parts to play in the training process, including clinical supervision (to a varying extent) and, crucially, assessment. In some training programmes potential difficulties are ameliorated to some extent by bringing in part-time staff with no role on the course other than to facilitate groups, but in the example we describe in more detail later, that of the programme of the Institute for Person Centred Learning (IPCL), this is not the case.

Rogers devoted an entire chapter in one of his earlier books to the training of counsellors and therapists (Rogers, 1951, pp. 429–78). Here, Rogers' basic philosophy is set out in some detail, but it can be summed up in a few sentences, 'There has been a steady trend away from technique, a trend which focuses upon the attitudinal orientation of the counselor. It has become apparent that the most important goal to be achieved is that the student should clarify and understand his own basic relationship to people, and the attitudinal and philosophical concomitants of that relationship. Therefore the first step in training client-centered therapists has been to drop all concern as to the orientation with which the student will emerge. The basic attitude must be genuine' (p. 432).

The chapter, however, pays scant attention to the possibilities of group work as an aid to training. There is some discussion of group and sub-group discussion periods, and their outcomes were noted as being of benefit, for example, 'Throughout this period there were insightful learnings which often struck the group member with the full force of a therapeutic insight . . . As the group discussions continued, many members came to a decision-making and planning phase as they worked out the ways in which they would utilize their learnings in their work in their own community' (p. 448).

Had Rogers published this chapter in 1970 rather than 1951, we suspect the emphasis would have been dramatically different. By 1970, the date of publication of *Carl Rogers on Encounter Groups* (Rogers, 1970), Rogers had become convinced of the therapeutic possibilities of groups, and had realised their potency in helping people understand and experience the therapeutic attitudes and values for which he is best known. Rogers' interest in groups eventually led to him experimenting with group work in large international communities, conflict exploration groups, and in counsellor training contexts (see, for example, Barrett-Lennard, 1998, pp. 199–231). The IPCL programme, a British Association for Counselling (BAC) accredited learning programme in client-centred counselling and psychotherapy, is one example of a training course designed in collaboration with Rogers, and one where group work plays a central role in the training process. The remainder of this chapter concentrates on the authors' experience of running this training programme, focusing on the central role of the community group. It also draws heavily on the thoughts of a sample of participants – those who have actually experienced what IPCL offers. Some of their feedback is given as examples of how a person-centred training can be experienced in so many different ways, and not all feedback is uncritical.

The IPCL programme
A brief background
The IPCL counsellor training programme received its BAC accreditation in 1993. It is one of the few BAC accredited training courses that operates entirely residentially, consisting of six nine-day courses and fifteen residential weekends over three years. Numbers of participants have varied between fifteen and twenty-four. It is because of the residential nature of the programme that large and small groups can be offered that enable participants to immerse themselves fully in their learning over an extended period of time, an advantage not available to non-residential programmes with the same degree of intensity.

Training philosophy
The programme is predicated on a number of assumptions about the learning and

development process that are consistent with person-centred theory. For example, we make the assumption that people learn best when they are as fully involved in all aspects of their training as possible. In practical terms, this means that IPCL does not offer a pre-established curriculum organised into modules or units, but encourages participants to develop the programme collectively as the needs of individuals and groups become apparent. This process involves a heavy investment of time into building a learning community that is able to respond to individual and group needs as they arise. The planning and organising roles of the community group are, however significant, not the only purposes for which this group exists. Whilst issues of, for example, confidentiality, time-management and planning the use of other resources are vital, the potential for personal learning through participation in the group is immense. The functions of the community group vary with the needs of individuals and groups within it, and, at times, the community group may behave as an encounter group exploring personal development needs of individuals or relationships between individuals, whilst at other times it deals with the practical day-to-day issues of community living.

Our training approach is also inspired by the person-centred theoretical position that people can be trusted, in an environment in which the 'core conditions' are consistently present, to discover from within themselves the resources required for personal growth and development. We believe this to be as true of people in group situations as it is in individual client-centred counselling, and we are in complete agreement with John Wood when he stated, 'At its best, the whole, the community, can be a teacher for the seeker, a therapist for the client, provider of alternatives for the problem-solver, inspiration for the artist. The essence of its creative state may come not from one person, with answers, but out of a group of persons with questions, not fully realizing that a wisdom may be hidden in their searching' (Wood, 1984).

Our experience of large group working

The question of power
As in individual therapy, one of the first issues to be faced by group facilitators is that of power. In person-centred training groups, as in any other group, the power dynamic is likely to be most fragile, and therefore open to most manipulation, at the beginning of the relationship. Beginning participants often believe, as a result of past learning, that the facilitator really does know best and this makes it important that right from the start facilitators show a genuine respectful sensitivity for each participant's position. At this beginning stage, empathy for participants' fear, anxiety or any other feeling is essential. This is not the time for the facilitators to be suggesting that theories of phenomenology, or the actualising tendency, for example, should be on the agenda. The danger is that participants will accept these suggestions as a way of avoiding anxiety, and a power dynamic in favour of the facilitators will quickly be established. Similarly, the introduction by the facilitators of games or exercises may appear to deal with underlying feelings (and, in some measure may successfully achieve this), but it is likely that a similar

power dynamic will result, and the struggle for autonomy and independent and group-centred decision making will simply be postponed. There is, of course, a distinct parallel here with the process of individual client-centred counselling. In this context, the counsellor is focused on the present moment, learning how to understand this individual client from the client's unique frame of reference, and has no inclination to impose a structure on the counselling session, but to enable the client's agenda to emerge in its own time.

This approach does not always suit the learning style or expectations of every group member, and facilitators need to be aware that in not giving direction they can create discomfort for some participants:

> On the first day of the course – a nine-day intensive, there was no formal welcome or introduction of participants or facilitators to each other. We were left to stumble until someone said, somewhat angrily, that they wanted to know who was who and why everyone was there.
>
> I felt it would have been reassuring to have had some kind of 'ground rules' of how the group wanted to work together in order to get the best out of the group, each other and the course itself. Whilst I realise that we are all adults and have to take responsibility for our own behaviour and wants, for me, it often felt very like an encounter or est group and somewhat punitive.

However, as the group progresses, and the participants begin to establish what *they* see as *their* training needs, and they begin to trust that the facilitators mean what they say about people taking responsibility for their own learning, the likely result will be a genuine desire to invite the facilitators into the discussion to discover what they can offer which everyone in the group can then prioritise for their own needs. This is a distinct advantage of residential training over a period of time – small groups of participants and staff can be meeting to discuss theory for those who feel it to be appropriate, whilst others can be in skill-based groups, or self-development groups. The community group can, at a later time, discuss and share the learning from each of these groups. The idea that person-centred counsellor training is a collaborative activity in which each person's needs and contributions can be equally respected and valued can be established early on in the life of the learning community only if the facilitators genuinely trust that the process of the group will be in the direction of co-operation and creativity.

One participant expressed her experience as follows:

> I love the trust and acceptance involved in allowing us as trainees to provide the forum and context in which we learn. Trying to identify my needs has been a struggle but more meaningful than having someone tell me what I need to know.

And another wrote:

> There is a wonder (and frustration) at how the group process has a power and dynamic of its own, beyond the capacity of any one

member to control.

I have a sense of deep peace which is both inner and outer, that is, it has a spiritual or transpersonal dimension which happens at the end of especially deep sessions.

Issues of culture

A major advantage of residential programmes is that the mix of cultures present within the group has a wide variety of opportunities to become apparent, and for different ways of working and different values to find expression. (We define cultural issues here as including race, gender, disability, sexual preference, class and age, etc.) Once trust is established in a group, and there is a clear commitment that participants will stay together over an extended period of time, issues of prejudice and stereotyping, for example, can be confronted in ways that lead to greater self-awareness and awareness of others to the extent that workshops in 'race awareness' (for example) can rarely achieve. Although IPCL does devote weekends and parts of nine-day residentials to issues of difference, we find that cultural differences become woven into the fabric of the programme rather than made into 'special cases'. Because of this, issues of 'difference' often become part of the discussion in situations where such issues were not an explicit part of the activity. For example, working in triads to develop counselling skills, can lead to a discussion of the counsellor's unconscious prejudices.

On this theme, one participant wrote:

The group at times has been a comforting and scary and anxious place to be in. But the residential aspect offers an environment in which we can focus on the dynamics of interpersonal relationships with the difficulties, as well as the celebrations involved in the process of accepting differences between people. It has been challenging, fun and bloody hard work at the same time.

Working on issues of culture and difference can, of course, be risky and people can find themselves feeling attacked or confronted in unexpected ways. In these circumstances, as in all others, facilitators need to be able to maintain empathy and respect for all sides and, importantly, to allow time for issues to be explored fully and, if possible, resolved. In a residential setting there can be time for problems and difficulties between people to be absorbed and thought about, and the community group can, and often does, return to them in its effort to understand differences and accept them. One participant's experience of this is as follows:

Being verbally abused so violently, for being a man, that it took two sleepless nights re-finding my centre and deciding to stay with the group.

And the same participant:

Gradually making connections with a person I did not believe I could ever relate to meaningfully, resulting in that relationship becoming one of the deepest in the group for me.

Being present as hurt and anger, both from outside and within the group, moved from needing self-expression to mutual love and caring.

One of IPCL's explicit goals is to help create counsellors who are aware of, and sensitive to the needs of different people, groups and cultures, given that counsellors are almost inevitably going to work in multicultural settings. Opportunities to explore multiculturalism, and to confront personal prejudice often occur in learning communities that themselves are, in some measure, representative of our multicultural society. The 'opening up' of these issues in a learning community setting is the single most powerful way of meeting this goal, provided a trustworthy and supportive psychological environment has first been established.

Self-development in groups
We have already indicated our agreement with Mearns' idea that large, relatively unstructured groups provide rich opportunities for self-development – in person-centred terms the development of personal congruence. Whilst self-development includes dealing with issues concerning cultural and other differences, it also incorporates personal congruence as Rogers and others have defined it – the ability to admit experiencing into awareness without the need for distortion or denial. There are no exercises or structured experiences that can effectively confront issues of personal congruence with the same experiential power as engaging with others in large groups. Opportunities for honest feedback are more prevalent in this situation than any other. In other words, congruence cannot be 'taught' as if it were a skill, it has to be acquired through interaction with others and, through them, interaction with oneself.

Individual, personal therapy is, of course, also rich in opportunities for the development of congruence, but groups often provide a context that enables personal exploration in ways that are impossible in personal therapy. One participant remarked:

The group experience is incomparable to my experience of traditional teaching and learning, especially for counselling training, and I have confronted myself in a way that even personal therapy cannot provide.

Another, making a similar point expressed herself somewhat differently:
It reaches the parts one-to-one counselling does not seem to reach.
There is something about being witnessed and held by a group of people which can be immensely healing. It enabled me to let go of the idea of right and wrong, or one truth – having witnessed the different perceptions of the same event has increased my own confidence to voice and tease out my own views and feelings.

The community group can be, and is, experienced in many ways by different participants and differently by the same participant at different times. The power of the group to promote personal congruence is felt by many to be proportional to the degree of psychological safety the group promotes. The same participant, who at one time found the group to be 'immensely healing', was also aware that the experience could be very different:

> But a group can be a dangerous and potentially damaging place –
> caring and perceptive facilitation (by any group member/s) is essential
> as groups can behave in a way that an individual on their own does
> not. An individual can become a scapegoat – there is a fine line
> between a constructive challenge to a member's behaviour and the
> potential for damaging someone further.

That large groups can be experienced as powerful and frightening and, at the same time, or different times, as safe and growth promoting is nowhere better illustrated than in this next comment from one group participant. She illustrates vividly and movingly the enormous personal gains that can be made from courageously confronting oneself in a context that encourages deep personal exploration whilst attempting to offer the kind of environment that makes such a commitment to personal growth possible. We will conclude this section with her words, because no more seem necessary:

> I have found the process of being in a group-learning community
> the most painful, excruciating experience of my life. It fascinates
> me that I ever decided to join this kind of learning environment as it
> is exactly everything I have always run away from. I've spent from
> about the age of ten making sure I was not in groups of people or if
> I somehow found myself with more than two people in my presence
> I would be silent.
>
> It has been terrifying, has felt like life and death, has taken all of
> the resources I have to stay with it, and yet . . . I have felt less terrified,
> less anxious and less like I might die, the longer I have been able to
> stick it out. It still takes a huge amount of energy to bring myself to
> this group and stay in it but somewhere in me I am aware that it has
> been life-enhancing, even life-saving. I have faced the biggest fear
> in my life and somehow I keep coming back for more.
>
> In group work I have found the anxiety in me reach fever pitch,
> gut-churning fear for hours, but something in me has remained with
> it. I have spent an 'intensive' on this course throwing up before every
> group session. I can apply person-centred theory to my experience
> of group work by realising that I have been in a prolonged battle
> with my self-concept in which my actualising tendency is winning.
> I don't think I would want to repeat the experience of group work as
> regularly as I have made myself do by attending this course, because
> there is the fact that it has felt, and continues to feel, so extreme as if
> I am sticking needles in my eyes or something, but I can no longer

deny that working and learning in a group has radically changed how I feel about myself for the better.

Dilemmas for the facilitators

The facilitators' (or trainers') roles are, of course, complex. They have responsibilities both to the group and to the wider counselling community and, eventually, to ensure that clients receive safe, ethical and effective counselling. Whilst there is no detailed predetermined curriculum, there are requirements for counsellor training made explicit in both BAC's and IPCL's documentation that cannot simply be ignored. The staff problem revolves around how to introduce these requirements and ensure they are fulfilled without imposing them artificially and whilst respecting the needs of the group and individuals within it. People learn at different rates and in different ways, and some of the time individuals are open to personal learning and growth, other times to issues of theory and at other times to the development of skills. If the facilitators see this as their problem, they are likely to impose a structure on the group that reflects their level of anxiety, and which may not be (indeed, is unlikely to be) an appropriate structure for the group. The time spent in building a learning community able to make wise choices of direction now becomes crucial. The facilitators can share their anxiety about fulfilling IPCL's and BAC's requirements openly and trust in the fact that participants have joined the course because they want to train as counsellors, and because they want their training to be recognised and respected by the wider community. The temptation for facilitators to take responsibility for the group is likely to be less compelling if the facilitators themselves have undergone a similar, intensive training, and have experienced for themselves the creativity and responsibility present within a training group in similar circumstances.

An important, and unavoidable, role for staff facilitators in counsellor training is to be engaged with the assessment process – both monitoring assessment throughout the course, and final assessment at the end of it. As indicated earlier, this can create some tensions as, for much of the time, the facilitators engage almost as equal participants (though with additional responsibilities), and for some of the time fulfil their assessment functions. There can be a temptation to avoid this conflict of roles by importing facilitators not involved with assessment to lead community or personal development groups. However, we believe that to separate the activity of personal and group development from other aspects of training in this way is to risk marginalising a central component of client-centred counsellor development. We support the view taken by Mearns (1997b), 'Personal development is core to the endeavour and it is vital that core staff can communicate and assist students in that regard. If the dual role of assessment creates problems then it is incumbent on the staff to find ways of solving the assessment problem rather than diminishing their training responsibility' (p. 117).

At IPCL we view assessment as an integral part of the programme, not as an issue somehow separate from it, although we have built in two occasions when assessment issues are made explicit. The first of these is a midway monitoring assessment in which each participant produces a self-assessment statement. Whilst each community group may decide to vary the format, in the past this statement has been discussed within peer groups. This has been an opportunity for the person to review her learning, receive feedback from colleagues and staff, identify strengths and weaknesses and to make decisions about what aspects of her development to concentrate on until the end of the programme. Participants referred to their personal journals and logs of counselling hours, supervision and personal growth to evaluate all aspects of their learning. The second is a formal end-of-programme assessment of skills, qualities, personal growth and theoretical understanding. Theory is assessed through written work, but the format for assessment of skills, qualities and personal growth is a matter for discussion within the community group. Previous groups have chosen to be assessed in peer groups (attended by a staff member). In these cases, participants had an hour to produce evidence to their peer group that they had acquired the necessary level of self-awareness, skill and understanding to offer effective and ethical counselling. Again, participants referred to their journals and professional logs and some produced a tape for discussion. The person being assessed played an active part in the decision-making process, and the staff member had no power to overturn a group decision.

It is essential that the community group is engaged centrally in the process of establishing the criteria for assessment and agreeing the format of the assessment process. Since some people find assessment threatening or anxiety provoking it is important that the community group spends time hearing, understanding and accepting these feelings. The facilitators need to play an active part in this process, helping individuals come to terms with their anxieties where they exist, and contributing to the development of a supportive and trusting environment. Our experience is that the community group will spend time developing clarity about the various roles to be fulfilled, the extent of staff responsibility, and clarifying criteria for assessment so that, whilst individuals may choose to produce evidence in a variety of ways, everyone works towards the same general criteria. Genuinely to involve the community group in this process underlines the staff trust in the responsibility of the group and individual members within it.

One set of feedback on assessment issues and processes illustrated the different ways in which people can perceive the same event. Feedback included, 'painful, but OK', 'very searching and exacting', 'tough but valuable', and, by contrast, 'not rigorous enough'.

The facilitator as a person
In the previous discussion we indicated the extent to which we believe the facilitators should engage in the group process as participants whilst not losing sight of their wider responsibilities. Facilitators are most likely to be effective when they are experienced by the group as exhibiting certain definable qualities and attitudes. These include the facilitators' valuing of the process of empathic understanding (and its communication), non-judgemental regard and personal congruence (or authenticity). These are not qualities or attitudes that can be

sustained unless they are genuinely and deeply held, and they cannot be experienced by others if the facilitators remain aloof from the process or separate themselves from the life of the learning community generally. Clearly there are some boundaries that need to be drawn, and facilitators need to be fully present within the community when it meets for training purposes, but they are unlikely to be involved to any great extent in the informal life of the community outside of meeting times.

We have found that being perceived by the community as a 'person' rather than simply as a staff member is an essential characteristic of person-centred training. We are impressed by the variety of styles and 'ways of being' of the numerous facilitators from the Continent and America with whom we have worked over many years. That there is not a single 'way of being' for person-centred practitioners that is expected by the approach, is a source of comfort and inspiration both to us as staff and to our participants. This extends from the different personal 'styles' of counselling, to the different personalities, characteristics and behaviour of staff members and 'guest' facilitators. We are reminded of one participant whose personal discovery that, 'It's OK to be me', was, for him, one of the most significant experiences of the whole programme.

The availability to the group of staff facilitators of different styles and approaches provides a richness and variety that is appreciated by participants. That different participants have different preferences is illustrated by some comments from group members:

> We have had facilitators who have seemed to provide a 'safety net'
> for the group by articulating and checking out issues that may have
> been left in limbo, perhaps where an individual may have been left
> with unresolved, unspoken issues that the group has not noticed or
> at least not outwardly acknowledged. These facilitators seem to have
> been highly sensitive to the group process. They have appeared to
> have been very 'present' and available in the group while generally
> not taking an actively verbal part unless (it seemed) they felt it
> important *for the well-being of the group* that they did so. They have
> 'taken care' of unattended business, or more accurately, brought
> unattended business back into awareness so that the group takes care
> of it. I think that this role was particularly important in the early
> stages of the group's development when creating safety was crucially
> important.
>
> A contrasting approach (or at least behaviour) has been to allow
> the group to go its own way, apparently trusting the process and the
> individuals to work things out in whatever way prove most useful to
> them. Such facilitation sometimes appeared to be unobtrusive to the
> point of near invisibility, and yet was certainly present when the
> group challenged and requested more input.

Another participant would prefer more active facilitation, and sometimes experiences the community group as unsafe, perhaps needing more guidance:

> The big group can also feel very threatening. When people decide
> they have something to say, it may be met with silence or sniffs to
> indicate, 'That was a waste of time'. It often seemed that members
> of the group felt unable to speak because they were afraid that what
> they said was not of sufficient importance to other members of the
> group.

Often much is made in discussions elsewhere about staff roles, of the need for
staff to 'model' the qualities and attitudes of the person-centred approach, but we
are somewhat suspicious of this attitude. Whilst participants do gain insight into
the meaning of the 'core conditions' through observing staff behaviour, and are
likely to experience, for example, empathic understanding from them, we are not
comfortable with the concept of 'modelling'. In our learning communities we do
not behave in certain ways because it is good 'modelling', but because we have
internalised these qualities and attitudes to the extent that they are natural and
genuine for us, at least to a significant and sustainable degree. We rarely, for
example, ask of each other, 'What is the person-centred thing to do?' when faced
with a difficulty or dilemma.

Conclusion
In this chapter we have tried to share some of our thinking and learning about the
place community groups have in the training of person-centred counsellors. There
is little empirical research of groups in this context, but much can be learned from
the limited literature on person-centred therapy groups and other kinds of groups
more generally. The richness of experience available in large groups is an essential
feature of effective person-centred counselling training, and we have found that
training groups can be trusted, provided an environment rich in the core conditions
is established, to find creative and growth-promoting directions for their members.
The experience of our participants, some of which is given above in their own
words, testifies to the extraordinary power of large groups to accelerate personal
growth and development in ways not available in personal counselling.

The fact that feedback, understanding and respect are available from a variety
of people in a group setting can mean that both very personal and wider cultural
issues can become available for exploration.

The role of staff facilitator is complex and demanding. It seems to us to be
vitally important that facilitators themselves need to have lived through these kinds
of groups before they can really trust in the group process, although we do know
remarkable exceptions to this.

We have perceived a general developmental sequence in groups – from anxiety,
defensiveness and uncertainty to openness, creativity and the ability to tolerate
and respect differences and similarities between and among people. Though this
general pattern is familiar to us, we are always surprised by the different ways in
which people use opportunities for growth, and excited by the potential for groups
to be very personal experiences as well as offering opportunities to explore wider

social and cultural issues.

As one of our participants put it:

> There is joy and pain in being fully in relationship with others. There is a mystical sense of being both completely individual and totally at one with others at the same time.

References

Barrett-Lennard, G. T. (1998) *Carl Rogers' Helping System.* London: Sage.

Brodley, B. and Merry, T. (1995) Guidelines for student participants in person-centred peer groups. *Person-Centred Practice, 3,* 2: 17–22.

Charleton, M. (1996) *Self-Directed Learning in Counsellor Training.* London: Cassell.

Irving, J. and Williams, D. (1996) The role of group work in counsellor training. *Counselling, 7,* 2.

Lyons, A. (1997) The role of group work in counselling training. *Counselling, 8,* 3.

Mearns, D. (1994) *Developing Person-Centred Counselling.* London: Sage.

Mearns, D. (1997a) *Person-Centred Counsellor Training.* London: Sage.

Mearns, D. (1997b) Achieving the personal development dimension in professional counsellor training. *Counselling, 8,* 2, 113–20.

Raskin, N. (1986a) Client-centred group psychotherapy, Part 1. *Person-Centred Review, 1,* 3: 272–90.

Raskin, N. (1986b) Client-centred group psychotherapy Part 2. *Person-Centred Review, 1,* 4: 389–408.

Rogers, C. R. (1951) *Client-Centred Therapy: Its Current Practice, Implications and Theory.* Boston: Houghton Mifflin.

Rogers, C. R. (1970) *Carl Rogers on Encounter Groups.* New York: Harper and Row.

Wood, J. K. (1984) Communities for Learning. In R. F. Levant and J. M. Shlien (eds.) *Client Centered Therapy and the Person-Centered Approach.* New York: Praeger.

Sexism, Gender Dynamics and the Person-Centered Approach

4

Peggy Natiello

Introduction

When I agreed to devote this chapter to a discussion of addressing sexism in person-centered groups, I decided to begin with an inquiry into current attitudes. The hostility that I encountered to the word itself, and the denial of its very existence, particularly among young adults, tempted me to discard it altogether.

In academic terms, the definition of sexism does not justify the negative reaction it evokes. Simply stated, sexism refers to prejudice, discrimination, and oppression based solely on gender. Lundy (1994) clarifies important distinctions between sexism and sex-role stereotyping. Sexism, he reminds us, gives license for economic, physical and emotional exploitation of women. One major destructive *outcome* of sexism is sex-role stereotyping, the practice of imposing gender-specific restrictions on men and women, thereby limiting their growth (p. 4). Those profound restrictions on roles and behavior that result from stereotyping have seriously deleterious effects on relationships between men and women – the very people who traditionally love, marry and raise children together. These effects threaten the social and personal arrangements in our culture, and have rendered constructive discussion of the issues extremely difficult.

Sexism is but one of many categories of inequality that are woven into the social construction of western culture. When we examine the history and institutions of western civilization, we inevitably find that socio-political arrangements create a breakdown of people into dominant and subordinate groups. The dominant group in the Euro-American culture has been composed mostly of Caucasian, heterosexual, Christian men from privileged backgrounds. This group has assumed the right to construct the concept of the *other* as a way of securing its own identity and maintaining its power and privilege. The *other* is always defined in terms of its relationship with the dominant group. Included in the other category, for instance, are women, homosexuals, the differently-abled, non-westerners, people of color, those from lower economic class, and the aged. Such a construction of society results in unequal and oppressive relationships. Edward Sampson (1993) calls this social construction a silent killer since it robs most human beings of genuine status in the world as well as the freedom to choose their opportunities, roles, and achievements.

It is difficult for most men to feel responsible for this construction, in that it is not the *conscious* intention of most individual men to dominate others. Yet men are often held accountable as part of the dominant group. This is especially true in terms of sexism. The renewed consciousness and anger of many women about the destructiveness of *their* subordinate status in society is often directed at individual men rather than at a system that impairs us in our quest to live fully and creatively.

Even more difficult are women's subsequent pleas to men for more emotional connection, more nurturing parenting, more shared responsibility around homemaking, more disclosing of deep feelings – all qualities that conflict with traditional masculine stereotyping. Women's pleas, as well as changing gender roles, have contributed to a serious identity crisis for many men, leaving them with feelings of defensiveness, confusion, anger and inadequacy (Farrell, 1986; Goldberg, 1977; Levant and Pollack, 1995; Levinson, 1996; Real, 1997).

Recently, in the burgeoning field of men's studies, scholars have begun to make us aware that gender-specific stereotyping for men is as destructive to emotional and psychological health and wholeness as it is for women. *Toward a New Psychology of Men* (Levant and Pollack, 1995) examines the injurious aspects of male socializing, and offers some compelling arguments for change. Terrence Real's *I Don't Want to Talk About It: The Legacy of Male Depression* (1997) considers the dire consequences of men's disconnection from feelings, particularly feelings of grief. The scattered circles of men who no longer view sexism and its consequences as simply a *women's* problem have raised my optimism about real changes in gender-powered relationships. Such men see the promise of more choice, freedom, vitality, respect for individual uniqueness, and fullness-of-being for themselves if sexism is eradicated. These and other significant insights coming out of male scholarship are underlining a simple fact: any culture informed by sexist values creates serious victimization for women *and* men alike.

In the following pages, I will take a brief look at the changing political trend in sexism since the late '60s, the personal damage associated with sexism and gender-specific stereotyping, and the consequent crisis in male/female relationships. I will then explore the radical political context of the person-centered group as a setting where gender conflict can be creatively addressed. In an effort to illuminate the possibilities for healing the painful rift and gross misunderstandings between men and women, and for liberating both sexes from the prevailing world-view of relationships, I will use examples from my work in person-centered groups that focused on gender issues.

Changing trends in sexism

Feminists in the '60s, '70s, and '80s raised hopes of radical transformation in the way men and women relate. They invited reflection on gender-related experience, and heightened awareness about gender-powered relations. They challenged partners, friends, families, associates and peers to bring new understanding and behavior into their relationships.

During those decades, women revitalized their struggles against oppression and against the internal and external constraints imposed by their gender-role identity. They found new support in facing the fear of social punishment for *not conforming* to the ideal stereotype of femininity on the one hand, and became increasingly aware of the self-destructiveness inherent in *conforming* to impossible gender norms. As they began to move into work outside the home, women discovered that 'having it all' meant *doing* it all. In addition to full-time jobs, they were still held accountable for home and children. Their raised consciousness led them to challenge men to set aside the prescribed behaviors of the male gender role and become different (often meaning more like women). These demands, in conflict with male stereotyping, threatened men's self-esteem and need for social approval. Levant (1995) has pointed out, in fact, that men are more severely punished for stepping outside their stereotypical behavior than are women, especially if they manifest qualities that are identified as more stereotypically feminine. Destabilizing gender roles during the '70s and '80s threw gender relations into crisis and threatened the entire fabric of our personal lives (Levinson, 1996; Rhodes, 1997).

In the '90s, feminist scholarship has continued to challenge the social construction of reality as it pertains to gender-powered relations. The major focus, however, has shifted to a more theoretical and institutional position. Beck (1997) has reported that major concerns of feminism in this decade are: the reform of existing patriarchal institutions; the reconstruction of history; critique of androcentric research and scientific methods; and the organization of social analyses.

This more abstract and theoretical direction, has been much less likely to arouse the *personal* passions that characterized the consciousness-raising movement of the previous two decades. In addition, caution has grown around any discussion of gender-powered relationships because of the hostility those issues raised in the '70s and '80s. Both situations have conspired to mask the pain, anxiety and fear generated by the upheaval in gender relations, and have seriously impaired the ability to grieve through the losses. Pleck (1997), in a discussion of men's difficulties with women's requests that they assume unfamiliar roles, has noted that every school of psychology respects grieving as 'the essential first stage in the resolution of trauma' (p. 20). It is this writer's belief that the attitudes toward sexism in the '90s have succeeded in driving underground the personal confusion, anger and grieving of men and women around gender-change.

Personal consequences of sexism and sex role stereotyping

No matter what the trend of gender studies, it is virtually impossible to deny that sexism and sex-role stereotyping are alive and well, and inflict negative consequences on women and men alike. Although most of my experience lies in the United States, I believe sexism remains intact world-wide.

Sexism issues for women
Those who insist that women have won equality are mired in denial. There have, indeed, been significant gains for *some* women, but some conditions for women have actually deteriorated (Levinson, 1996, p. 416). Research continues to demonstrate that women make less money than men for similar or equal work, and that equal work is often hard to get. Despite the narrowing financial gap, more than two-thirds of poverty-stricken adults are female. The story of institutional power remains grim. Ninety-two per cent of corporate executives and 85% of elected officials are male, even though women constitute over 50% of the voting force. Ninety per cent of women who have senior manager positions believe that men's and women's opportunities continue to be unequal (Rhodes, 1997). Essentially all political, religious, social and professional institutions are still directed by men even in traditionally female fields like primary education, nursing, and real estate.

On the domestic scene, the major burden of child-rearing and housework belongs to women, even when working full time. The growing number of women who are moving into traditional male work is in no way balanced by men assuming traditionally female work or responsibilities (Levant, 1995; Rhodes, 1997, p. 2). This creates serious voids in accountability – particularly for family life. Statistics of women who are victims of domestic violence continue to be harrowing. It is the 'leading cause of injury to women and claims an estimated four million victims annually' according to findings of the American Medical Association, the U. S. Surgeon General, and the Department of Justice (Rhodes, 1997, p. 108).

In the legislative arena, hopes around many hard-fought feminist battles in the United States have been dashed. The Equal Rights Amendment did not win approval; affirmative action has been overturned; and reproductive freedom has been seriously curtailed (Rhodes, 1997). Although new laws exist on the books to protect minority rights, there has been growing acknowledgement that eliminating obstacles to equality is one part of the story – enforcing compliance is another (Katzenbach and Marshall, 1998).

Feminine stereotypes of gentleness, submissiveness, caretaking, attractiveness, and emotionality among others are still in place (Friday, 1996; Levinson, 1996; Pipher, 1994). Assertive, powerful, too-visible women continue to be punished for not upholding the ideal norms of femininity. The hazards of claiming personal power are most clearly demonstrated by the lives of prominent women who make the news. Hillary Rodham Clinton has been persistently criticized for being politically powerful. She has had to redirect her attention away from national and international policy to focus on family affairs – a more acceptable arena of commitment for women. Anita Hill's accusations of sexual harassment against Clarence Thomas, then nominee to the Supreme Court, were turned back on her. Members of the all-male investigating committee suggested that she was mentally unbalanced, a bitter rejected woman, and a pawn of political women's groups. Several years after he won his appointment to the Supreme Court and she was portrayed as a liar, however, polls indicate that the majority of Americans believe in the truth of her accusations. The censure that these two women have suffered for breaching the expectations of their feminine role illuminates what Joseph Pleck (1981) refers to as gender role strain.

Sex-role stereotyping issues for men
Interest in men's experience is growing, and some scholars are examining men's development in terms of gender. They are uncovering the very high price men pay for the dominant status they are *supposed* to enjoy but rarely feel (Goldberg, 1977; Kammer, 1994; Keen, 1991; Levant and Pollack, 1995; Real, 1997). Recognition that normative masculinity as a social construction is impossible to achieve without impairing the psychological, physical, and emotional health and wholeness of those who try is becoming increasingly obvious.

For those men who attempt to conform to rigid masculine norms, the damage to self often includes the inability to grieve, workaholism, detached fathering, difficulty of emotional intimacy, impersonal sex, fierce competition, neglected physical health, and more (Levant and Pollack, 1955). The consequences for *over-conforming* can be more severe, even leading to individual and social destructiveness manifested by chemical addiction, suicide, violence, oppression, sexual harassment, misogyny, and pornography (Brooks and Silverstein, 1995; Keen, 1991; Levant and Pollack, 1995; Pleck, 1995; Real, 1997). At the present time, President Clinton stands accused of sexual harassment and aggression toward a number of women. No matter what the outcome of the current investigations, the position of power held by Clinton, the relative social powerlessness of the women on whom his attention settled, and the alleged use of these women as sexual objects reflect the sexualized attitudes that often result from expectations inherent in male socialization. Brooks and Silverstein (1995) describe these outcomes of exaggerated male gender norms as 'the dark side of masculinity' (p. 280).

Those men who do *not* conform are more blatantly criticized by society than are women who turn away from their gender expectations. Taunts of 'wimp' and 'fag' plague the developmental years of young boys who demonstrate such qualities as gentleness, sensitivity, studiousness, and disinterest in sports (Krugman, 1995). Adult men who do not demonstrate machismo are generally considered less successful than those who do. The dilemma for men in the '90s, whether they conform to normative masculine standards or not, is that they cannot win.

The male experience, as well as the female experience, needs to be heard with tenderness and empathy in order to begin an authentic healing dialogue between men and women. Yet it is difficult to dialogue about sexism because most men are unaware of the suffering of self and others that results from male norms. Only when men begin to comprehend the price they pay for maintaining male norms, and talk about the pain and confusion associated with their gender-specific socializing will they receive a compassionate and healing response.

In the meantime, criticism of the traditional male role is often mistaken for criticism of men themselves. When that happens, men understandably become defensive, push away any discussion of gender, and are unable to hear women's appeals for change. Any gender-role discussion quickly becomes a *women's* problem, and the conversation is repressed both by men who feel unjustly accused, and by women who are afraid of men's disapproval and anger. More and more, men and women behave as though none of this anguish between them is really happening. The mantle of denial grows thicker.

With women's anger over their subordinate position, and men's defensiveness about being blamed for the ills of the world, it seems impossible for a civil empathic dialogue around gender arrangements to take place. At the very least, it seems impossible in a setting that mirrors the prevailing socio-political climate and dominant/subordinate arrangements between women and men.

Person-centered groups: One step toward resolution
The person-centered approach offers a radically different view of relationships – one that challenges the presently-held assumptions of domination and subordination. Person-centered communities are designed to be without hierarchy, designated leaders, or predetermined agendas. Certain norms of femininity like receptivity, empathy and emotional connectedness are highly prized, as are certain norms of masculinity like directness, self-responsibility, assertiveness and personal power. This approach holds that all persons and groups can equally resolve their own problems, make choices about how to use themselves, and contribute to continuing social emergence. Differences are valued and viewed as enriching the whole, rather than repressed or seen as deviant. In this radically different socio-political culture, participants are free to reclaim parts of themselves that have atrophied as a result of gender socialization. They are encouraged, even challenged, to find their authentic voices and to expand their ways of being in the world.

Such a challenge is immense. Gender stereotypes are so deeply embedded in the psyches of men and women that discarding stereotypical attitudes and behaviors is emotionally and psychologically wrenching and is likely to take years to eradicate. Experiences in person-centered groups focused on gender, however, hold much promise for change.

In the following pages, I will describe work that a colleague, Curtis Graf and I undertook in order to understand and invite dialogue about gender-powered relations in the context of person-centered groups, large and small. The themes and hypotheses that follow were identified consistently by both of us over years as participant-observers.

The largely middle-class groups were composed of mostly Caucasian heterosexual Americans, with from two to five homosexuals in each gathering. Ages ranged from early twenties to mid-seventies, and group size from as small as 12 to one group of 150. The total number of participants was approximately 320. The meetings took place between 1980 and 1991 and lasted for as few as three days and as many as ten weekends during the year. Each group had a clearly defined gender focus.

The experiences were always full of tension, insight, frustration, anger, pain and celebration. Participants who entered without awareness of gender-specific issues, became appalled as victims of abuse told stories of rape, homophobia, child molestation, hampered professional advancement, father-hunger, forced athletic activity and performance-enhancing drugs resulting in permanent injury. It was not long, however, before most participants identified some gender-specific experiences and limitations in their own lives, as well as in the group processes, and underwent observable changes in behavior.

What person-centered groups have taught us about gender

In keeping with the belief that persons will find their own way to deal with problems as well as their own solutions, the person-centered process was not *directed* by the facilitators. The participants in every group, however, quickly and invariably developed their own model of working alternately in single-sex and mixed-sex groups. This model demonstrated that women explore their gender-related experiences most deeply and freely in the company of other women, and men in the company of other men. The single-sex groups provided insight into struggles with persons of the same sex as well as the deep emotional wrenching of both genders as they confronted their normative stereotypical socializing and attempted to reclaim aspects of self that had atrophied.

The mixed groups, on the other hand, illuminated sexist patterns of behavior, the intensity of hurt and anger between men and women, and the transformative process of healing. Despite the uniqueness of each group, the themes and processes described below were consistent with one exception. In that group, anger, pain and defensiveness overtook the experience and were never resolved.

Experiencing the pain amid anger

Initially, the mixed-group meetings were characterized by expressions of discomfort about the subject of gender and peppered with friendly jokes. Early in these mixed groups, a crisis around sexism inevitably arose. It was often triggered by a political discussion, a disclosure from someone's past, or an interaction in the group that carried traces of sexism. In one group, it began when a woman expressed outrage at the murder of female university students in Canada by a male student, and one of the male participants jumped to the murderer's defense. In another it was precipitated by two men who felt rejected by a woman participant they accused of being seductive. Inevitably, intense feelings of anger, hurt, fear, blame and defensiveness erupted and placed the climate of the group in jeopardy.

There was always an effort on the part of some to deny or trivialize these feelings. Recurring experience, however, revealed that anger and pain around dominant/subordinate gender arrangements and changing role expectations *always* existed, even when below the conscious level. Negative feelings always surfaced in the safety of the person-centered climate *if* true openness was fostered and *if* feelings were attended to when they were voiced. Jean Baker Miller (1990) pointed out that anger, creatively addressed, can be a potent healing force in relationships.

In contrast, however, when feelings were repressed or ignored, the group became immobilized and personal connections became inauthentic. Indeed, until all the hurt and angry feelings were addressed, relationships remained superficial, resistant and unresolved. The deep wounds inevitably inflicted in a sexist culture could not be healed until they were acknowledged and grieved. We learned that the intensity of wounding around gender relationships was not for the faint-hearted, and that ignoring it simply fuelled the fire.

Defensiveness and the development of empathy

At the point where anger surfaced in the mixed group, the relationships between men and women disintegrated into the stereotypical coping patterns that threatened to lock the two genders into dominant and subordinate roles.

The men generally withdrew emotionally and sometimes physically from women's anger. 'I don't need this', 'I feel punished', or 'I don't know what their problem is' were typical of remarks that accompanied their increasingly passive stance. The more intense the feelings, the more withdrawn the men became until almost all the interaction in the mixed group was among the women. As the men pulled out of the group process, the women experienced male silence as controlling.

Withdrawal and silence are often behaviors that men choose when faced with the threat of emotional connection, especially hostile connection. Although this dynamic was frustratingly familiar to most women, men generally had little or no understanding of the way their behavior interfered with dialogue. Most of the men in these groups had difficulty connecting empathically with their deep inner experience, in that they have been taught not to *feel*. It was at this point that the mixed group reached an impasse which inevitably led to a request from one or more participants to separate into men's and women's groups. Thereafter until near the end of the meeting, participants moved back and forth between single-sex and mixed-sex groups.

Dialogue in the men's group helped to clarify the feelings and resistance the men had in reaction to the crisis in the mixed group. More often than not, they talked about what Bergman (1995) described as male relational dread. He reported that, in the intensity of relationship with women, men often experience an overwhelming sense of defensiveness and incompetence that gets mixed up with their perceived pressure to respond to women. When confronted with women's anger in the person-centered mixed communities, men generally felt blamed and consequently withdrew. They expressed disgust at their apparent abandonment by the women who had reacted to some issue of sexism, and at the increasing coldness and emptiness of the climate. They preferred discussions in all-male groups to any emotional encounters with women, although, to this point, most of the men had not experienced empathy and deep listening from other men.

The women's responses to the same crisis were varied. Some women experienced anxiety because they felt responsible for the conflict and resulting anger in the mixed group. By expressing negative feelings, especially anger, they had defied the feminine norms of cooperation, docility and niceness. It was common for their behavior to incur the anger of men, but they were surprised to lose the support of some women. The unfolding group process revealed that this withdrawal of support had several origins: distress about losing the alliance with men, anxiety about unfulfilled role expectations and their own unexplored anger. Such responses were consistent with the behavior of the oppressed as described by the Brazilian revolutionary Paulo Friere. He pointed out that the struggle of subordinates to liberate themselves was resisted often by their own group. Some subordinates were fearful of freedom and preferred the 'security of conformity . . . to the creative communion produced by . . . the pursuit of freedom' (Friere, 1970, p. 32).

Deepening awareness amid self-responsibility
As men and women continued to explore their gender-related experience with others of the same sex, their self-awareness and self-empathy deepened. Men grappled with the loss of some of their privilege as gender roles have become less rigidly defined. Some expressed anger at the resultant changes in their homes and the new expectations from primary partners. Many acknowledged and began to address the aggression they found within themselves toward women and gay men. Bonding was often established around their mutual lack of connection to, and mentoring by, fathers. They explored their anger at women in the group who had withdrawn emotional support. They often discovered the double-bind of needing the nurturing that women usually provide and not being skilled at giving it to one another. Some continued to see the anger of the women as a 'vicious attack'. The understanding they received from other men, however, helped them to move periodically back into the mixed group where they were increasingly able to express their feelings.

In the women's group, on the other hand, some were confronting their feelings of abandonment by other women and recognizing the competition among themselves. Some were struggling with the identity crisis triggered by not nurturing and soothing the men. Women recognized the indirect and manipulative style of expressing anger often associated with feminine socializing and internalized oppression. They felt intense anger about their subordinate position in intimate and professional relationships, and their dependence on men for approval and esteem. The more they were able to break through the denial of inequality with male partners, fathers and bosses, the more women were able to understand the terrible fear of speaking in their own voice and the toll those relationships had taken on their self-confidence. Several women voiced their strong and previously unacknowledged homosexual yearnings which evoked fear, especially for those who were married with children. As both groups began to face squarely some of the personal consequences of living in a sexist culture, the focus was taken off the other gender, enabling empathy to grow for the self-experience.

Each time the men and women returned to the mixed group, they brought a greater understanding of their own gender-related issues, and a heightened ability to hear and deal with the other gender's pain. As single-sex groups grew more open and honest, most participants' behavior changed dramatically. They moved from defensiveness and disconnection, through increasing awareness, self-confrontation and grief, to reconnection, and finally to celebration of the positive socialized characteristics that distinguish their own gender. Self-acceptance and self-validation fostered respect and empathy for the other gender and paved the way for healing.

Healing by grieving together

The healing process in the mixed group was almost always advanced when one of the men was genuinely able to disclose *his* pain around gender socialization. In one meeting, it began with a man who grieved about the anger and violence he felt toward women. He and one of the women who had touched into rage about male violence wept together. Another time, it was the voice of a young man who told the group that he used to pray as a child that he would die before he was old enough to go to war. A middle-aged man, very successful in his own life, confessed his strong attraction to, but fear of, powerful women. 'When I'm with a powerful woman, I feel the roll of fat around my waist and the dirt under my fingernails.' Moments like those shifted the sexist rift dramatically. The search for *whose fault it all is* flowed into a stream of empathy between and among men and women as they confronted the truth of their experiences; expressed grief at the deeply embedded behaviors, attitudes, prejudices and fears that result from their socializing; articulated them genuinely; and heard themselves and each other with genuine compassion.

From this time until the meetings came to an end, interactions around gender were generally marked with mutual understanding, deep compassion, healing dialogue and good humor – even hilarity. Each person seemed more aware and accepting of gender issues, and, hence, much less vulnerable to being blocked by those issues. There were marked changes in men's and women's behavior toward one another. Participants identified the change as growing out of self-compassion, as well as compassion for the experience of the opposite sex. Understanding by men and women that they had forfeited personal development by over-conforming to stereotypical ideals became clear. They began to see that the definition of certain characteristics as positive for only *one* gender was grossly inaccurate. Women experimented with more directness and autonomy; men with more empathy and self-disclosure. Celebration of self and gentle encouragement from others often accompanied these experiments into new behavior. Whereas in the beginning, men tended to dominate the organizational and theoretical process and women tended to dominate the emotional interactions, a new balancing of participation became evident. The way was now open for more whole, egalitarian and cooperative relationships.

Conclusion

March 1998: *Two boys, one 11 and the other 13, opened fire on an Arkansas schoolyard filled with children and teachers. They killed four girls and a pregnant teacher and injured 11 others. According to reports, the motive was anger at an*

11 year-old female student who did not want to be the 13 year-old's girlfriend. 'No girl is going to break up with me,' he is reported to have said.

This horrifying crime happened during the time I was writing this chapter. It reflects the mood of violence and hostility that plagues efforts to change gender roles and stereotypical expectations. It gives credibility to Levinson's (1996) statement that during the '90s, 'The level and intensity of gender conflict have risen . . . We live in a state of gender warfare . . .' (p. 417). Awareness that oppression, prejudice and anger drive even our children sends a powerful wake-up call about the urgency of promoting healing dialogue between, and among, men and women.

The person-centered group experience is a fertile field in which to begin that dialogue. Rogers (1980) has already set the precedent for facilitating person-centered meetings in fiercely-divided groups like the Irish warring among themselves and the South Africans living under apartheid. He says,

> In the presence of the facilitative attitude created by staff and by many participants, individuals gradually begin to *hear* one another, and slowly to understand and to respect. The atmosphere becomes a *working* atmosphere, both in the large and the small groups, as people begin to delve into themselves and their relationships (p. 193).

Experience with gender-focused groups reinforces the effectiveness of person-centeredness in dealing with conflict between men and women and underlines some crucial ingredients for healing. Essential elements of that work follow.

- Genuineness, empathy and positive regard facilitate the safety necessary for the expression of intense feelings around gender and their resolution. Gender-sensitivity and the courage of facilitators and some participants can counteract the anger, fear and denial often associated with these primal issues.
- Single-sex groups help men and women raise gender-specific awareness, express pain and anger, gain support for their feelings and take responsibility for themselves.
- Mixed-gender groups provide a microcosm for recognition of sexist patterns, and encourage experimentation with new behaviors that have atrophied in over-conforming to gender socialization.
- Self-responsibility rather than blame is crucial to healing. To project one's anger and pain onto the other gender is to assume a victim position and is counterproductive.
- Feelings must be expressed fully and freely, and heard empathically for authentic reconnection to take place.
- Grieving together is a major step toward healing. 'I know now that to know pain is to be capable of suffering, and to suffer is to be capable of empathy with others,' writes Steven Shapiro (1984, p. 214).

Avoidance of gender issues, especially in the face of today's violence and hurt, is dangerous. 'Wars are not caused by conflict,' says Michael Meade (in Kammer,

1994), 'but rather by the avoidance of conflict.' Direct engagement with the conflict, and the resulting grief, changes the gender 'war' (Levinson, 1996) into a cultural problem we all face, and opens the way for understanding, mutual respect, genuine communion in primary and professional relationships and families, and the reclamation of aspects of self that have atrophied in the socializing process.

References

Beck, R. (1997) Interdisciplinary Feminist Contributions. Unpublished doctoral paper.

Bergman, S. (1995) Men's psychological development: A relational perspective. In R.Levant and W. Pollack (eds.), *Toward a New Psychology of Men* (pp. 68–90). New York: Harper Collins.

Brooks, G.and Silverstein, L. (1995) Understanding the dark side of masculinity: An interactive system model. In R. Levant and W. Pollack (eds.), *Toward a New Psychology of Men* (pp. 280–333). New York: Harper Collins.

Farrell, W. (1986) *Why Men Are the Way They Are*. New York: McGraw Hill.

Farrell, W. (1993) *The Myth of Male Power: Why Men are the Disposable Sex*. New York: Simon and Shuster.

Friday, N. (1996) *The Power of Beauty*. New York: Harper Collins.

Friere, P. (1970) *Pedagogy of the Oppressed*. New York: Seabury Press.

Goldberg, H. (1977) *The Hazards of Being Male. Surviving the Myth of Masculine Privilege*. New York: NAL-Dutton.

Goldberg, H. (1991) *What Men Really Want*. New York: Signet.

Kammer, J. (1994) *Good Will Toward Men*. New York: St. Martin's Press.

Katzenbach, N. and Marshall, B. (1998) *Not Color Blind: Just Blind*. New York Times Magazine, Feb. 22, pp. 42–5.

Keen, S. (1991) *Fire in the Belly*. New York: Bantam Books.

Krugman, S. (1995) Male development and the transformation of change. In R. Levant and W. Pollack (eds.), *Toward a New Psychology of Men* (pp. 91–126). New York: Harper Collins.

Levant, R. and Pollack, W. (1995) Introduction. In R. Levant and W. Pollack (eds.), *Toward a New Psychology of Men* (pp. 1–8). New York: Harper Collins.

Levinson, D. (1978) *The Seasons of a Man's Life*. New York: Knopf.

Levinson, D. (1996) *The Seasons of a Woman's Life*. New York: Knopf.

Lundy, B. (1994) *Talking Man to Man about Sexism*. Bibliographical information incomplete.

Meade, M. (1994) Foreword. In J. Kammer, *Good Will Toward Men*. New York: St. Martin's Press.

Miller, J. B. and Surrey, J. (1990) *Revisioning Women's Anger: The Personal amid the Global* (Stone Center Working Paper Series, Work in Progress No. 43). MA. Wellesley College, Stone Center.

Pipher, M. (1994) *Reviving Ophelia: Saving the Selves of Adolescent Girls*. New York: Ballantine Books.

Pleck, J. (1981) *The Myth of Masculinity*. Cambridge: The MIT Press.

Pleck, J. (1995) The gender role strain paradigm: An update. In R. Levant, and W. Pollack (eds.), *Toward a New Psychology of Men* (pp. 11–32). New York: Harper Collins.

Real, T. (1997) *I Don't Want to Talk About It: The Legacy of Male Depression*. New York: Simon and Schuster.

Rhodes, D. (1997) *Speaking of Sex: The Denial of Gender Inequality*. Cambridge: Harvard University Press.

Rogers, C. R. (1980) Learnings in large groups: Their implications for the future. In *A Way of Being* (pp. 316–39). Boston: Houghton Mifflin.

Sampson, E. (1993) *Celebrating the Other*. Boulder, CO: Westview Press.

Shapiro, S. A. (1984) *Manhood: A New Definition*. New York: G. P. Putnam and Sons.

Experiencing Diversity

5

Ruth Sanford

Preface

I acknowledge the assistance of Ed Bodfish in preparing the materials for this chapter on experiencing diversity. He began as a participant and became more and more a colleague in the workshops which are held annually in October. Increasingly, his questions, his recommendations and his critical comments have been of great value in the preparation of this paper.

Origin

Our quest began in 1984 at a person-centered workshop in Mexico City at the Universidad Iberoamericano. Carl Rogers and I had been invited to participate on a panel composed of practitioners in a wide range of therapies, all the way from Freudian analysis through Neo-Freudian to behaviorist and one or two others. Carl Rogers and I represented the humanistic approach or, more specifically, the person-centered approach (evolved from client-centered therapy) applied to groups as well as individuals.[1] Various members of the panel had discussed among themselves at some length the value they placed on the fee which they charged and there was some 'shoptalk' among the analysts and others. When we had finished the presentations, a Mexican woman social worker in Mexico City stood up and made an impassioned plea which ended in a question, 'I have heard all this about the various therapies and fees. I would like to know what are you doing to take care of the needs of the thousands of people who cannot afford private psychotherapy?'

---

[1] For a discussion of some of the history see my article 'An Inquiry into the Evolution of the Client-Centered Approach to Psychotherapy' in Zeig, J. editor (1987) *The Evolution of Psychotherapy.* New York: Brunner/Mazel, and the introduction by Jeffrey Zeig which discusses elitism.

There was a pause. Then she addressed her question to me. I was taken completely by surprise and for what seemed like a long moment I could not find words. Then, as nearly as I can describe it, I heard a voice in my mind saying, 'Elitism. We must go beyond elitism.' I then told of the common practice among client-centered or person-centered therapists to determine the fee by reaching a decision about the fee with the client as partner in the decision. I know many person-centered therapists who did not turn a client away because of an inability to pay. I referred to the fact that in our workshops we had found that many of the participants responded either at the workshop or later with expressions like, 'You have changed my life,' or, 'It had a lasting effect on me and I am keeping in touch with others whom I met at the workshop.' I also referred to the fact that many times one half-hour demonstration therapy session between Carl and a volunteer client was sufficiently powerful to call forth a comment such as, 'It changed my life.'

First steps
The idea of departing from the usual or traditional pattern of person-centered workshops evolved rather slowly during the summer of 1993. I think I became aware that for the most part the participants in person-centered workshops were white, middle-class professionals or students with a sprinkling of others who were seeking an opportunity for personal growth. At the beginning we had considered an experiential workshop acquainting newcomers with the concepts of the person-centered approach. We had also considered a learning experience or training program in the New York area. The third possibility of a diversity workshop came to the fore in the August of 1993. The need for going beyond elitism came up at the end of the 1992 Association for the Development of the Person-Centered Approach (ADPCA) meeting in Redwood City, California, where the need for more outreach to various minority groups was discussed. We decided that those who had expressed interest at the ADPCA conference and others who had experience in person-centered group work, both within and outside the New York City area, should be included in the planning. Three persons from Kutztown, Pennsylvania and six from the New York/Long Island area were present at the August and September meetings. In October, two persons from the Massachusetts and Connecticut area were added.

Initially in June, the intent was to set a date for the workshop in November, but as our objective became clearer, we realized that more time was needed – probably late spring or early summer would be realistic. It became clear that a long preparation period made heavy demands on the time of members of the planning group. At this point, attendance at the monthly meetings fluctuated. Individuals determined they were making the choice of staying in the planning group or withdrawing because they were unable to make the commitment. In a real sense the planning group was self-selected; no one person was in charge. The process was time consuming.

One objective was to bring together a group of genuinely interested persons who themselves represented diversity of background. We decided to meet one Sunday each month at a central meeting place almost equidistant from Pennsylvania and Massachusetts. We also felt the need to meet for one two-day period to know each other better in depth. We had to feel our way because no one of our group had ever deliberately set out to bring together the highest degree of diversity possible. It was a process of exploration and discovery.

Illustrated learnings
The learnings from the Experiencing Diversity workshops 1994–1998 we have selected to illustrate are:
* Dissension in the planning group is mirrored in the workshop.
* Harmony in the planning group is mirrored in the workshop.
* Make it clear you want to hear each person.
* The importance of commitment in the planning group.
* The deeper the exchange, the greater the binding.

What I have experienced with Experiencing Diversity workshops also holds true for large and small groups. I find that the learnings from the Experiencing Diversity workshops are compatible with those from all PCA groups both large and small. (See the chapter in this volume 'A Brief History of My Experience of the Development of Small and Large Group Work in the PCA'.)

Dissension in the staff is mirrored in the group
In contrast to Experiencing Diversity 1998 our experience in 1997 demonstrated the effect that disharmony in the staff resulted in such disharmony in the group that some participants did not return in 1998 because they felt unsafe and others left with heavy hearts and many conflicts unresolved.

Harmony in the staff is mirrored in the group
A staff member's suggestion that we meet less often but for longer weekend meetings rather than more single day meetings was vital to the harmony and unity of the staff in 1998. That we were able to overcome the one bump in the road of an otherwise deep and joyful meeting was due in large part to the harmony achieved at the staff meetings throughout the year. More details about this can be found in the section below discussing *Make it clear you want to hear each person*.

The work on the beautiful collage and brochure done in all the colors of the rainbow gave the planning group a momentum it never lost. The statement, 'celebrate differences' along with similarities in the Experiencing Diversity 5 brochure set a tone for the workshop.

Make it clear you want to hear each person
In two workshops, one with Carl and one by myself, I have experienced consciously saying something that changed the direction of the meeting.

One group in Moscow had been a violent occasion where facilitators were confronted with doing something after much vituperation. People had been screaming at each other and our repeated appeals for participants to speak one at a time because we wanted to hear each one were ignored. At the end of the evening session the facilitators agreed to ask the participants to sit silently for five minutes, not to speak to each other as they left, and to return the following morning at nine o'clock. Next day the participants began listening to one other and the atmosphere became increasingly positive.

In the closing session of Experiencing Diversity 5 (1998) to everyone's surprise one member of the staff suddenly exploded in such anger that newcomers were feeling threatened. They had been promised that this was a place where they could feel safe. One by one, members of the group familiar with the PCA, not newcomers, expressed their feelings – of being 'terrorized by you'; 'in your words I heard the rage of my father when I was a child'; 'I see you as a man filled with rage'; 'maybe it's the little boy in you who didn't get hugged enough by his mother.'

I could hear that the younger, less experienced people were closing up, afraid to speak. They were young people, some of them from backgrounds of deprivation, and the fear and anger of the adults who had invited them to 'a safe place to be yourself' was evident. At this point I as one of the facilitators was on the verge of tears myself. I felt it would be impossible to settle all those differences in the last hour. So I expressed my strong feeling,

> I would like the persons involved to come together at the close of
> the workshop to work out their differences and that we turn our
> attention to those who had felt attacked. I had hoped we could turn
> our attention in the last hour to those who had been afraid to speak,
> to those who had felt unsafe.

We took time to acknowledge the many strong and positive contributions of the person who had exploded. Then the unsafe ones spoke and the meeting closed on a very rich and upward note. We ended in close concentric circles singing *Kumbaya* with workshop variants for refrains where the last was, 'See you here again next year!'

Much of that night and the following morning the facilitative staff involved worked out their differences. The person who had exploded said I had done the right thing when I said I wanted to hear the silent ones. Then during final farewells I reached for my bag. Another member of the staff said, 'That's my bag.' I said, 'I guess we have to sort out our own baggage, don't we?' We laughed and ended on a note of harmony.

After this workshop at least six groups of people (from Canada, Michigan, Chicago, Arizona, California, and Connecticut) felt strongly energized to return home and start their own Experiencing Diversity workshops in their neighborhoods.

There was a general feeling expressed that this was the richest Experiencing Diversity workshop of the five years. One of the staff members who had been strongest in attracting young people to the workshop expressed more strongly than ever before her dedication to continue doing so.

Using the principle that the participants or clients are the authority on the experience, I quote a letter from a participant:

> The Experiencing Diversity Workshop was a very positively moving experience for me from the warm invitation, to the most incredible representation of feelings and ideas expressed across the lifespan, across ethnicity and race, across economic and social classes, across philosophical and political lines.

The importance of commitment in the planning staff

There were many doers on the planning staff, dedicated enough to execute large tasks steadily and well, from the brochure to fund-raising, recruiting, accounting, housing arrangements, or transportation.

The deeper the exchange the greater the binding

The deepest exploration of celebrating differences occurred on the second day of Experiencing Diversity 1998 when several African-American participants shared in depth the pain and disappointment they had suffered in finding their place in the life and culture of the US. So intense was the involvement that the group continued with it all afternoon through the time allotted for free activities. Close binding was evident.

Members of our diverse staff speak for themselves

A 'This is a story of my experiencing diversity growing up in a beautiful small town in Virginia surrounded by mountains, where everyone lived all over no matter what their race or economic status and where everyone interacted with each other even before the days of school integration. We were a Black family of four boys and four girls. My mother was a school teacher who stopped teaching when her children were born and my father was a coal miner who had also been a baseball player and railroad man after growing up on a farm.

Diversity started for me soon after birth. I was born on June 9th and my next-door neighbor, Buddy, who is a Caucasian male, was born June 21st. He had a female first cousin who was born a couple of months before us in April. We all played together and since then mixed with the other kids on the street. Being in such proximity, whenever their family had problems we worried about them, and whenever there was sickness in our family they were there for us. When my mother needed a cup of sugar, it was over to Buddy's house I would go.

Whenever my mother made us stay in the yard, Buddy would be at the fence playing through [it] and over it.

Since the entire town had similar situations, when we were old enough to venture out into the community, we met new friends and continued to play together. When the city established a Little League, it too was integrated and we were on the same team or we played against each other. My two brothers and I were chosen for the Green team because the manager of that team worked at the same place as my father so even though he did not know us, he felt he was getting good players because of who my father was to him. We were good players because my father had played semi-pro baseball and taught us to play.

This led to us getting to know kids all over town. So we were at each other's houses all of the time. Wherever [we were when] the 12 o'clock whistle blew is where we had lunch. My parents were caring and kind people who made friends with anyone and everyone so I was often accepted by people I may have not known but who knew my parents.

As wonderful as these experiences were there were injustices that happened. The school system was segregated. The local labor pool did not include us. The only professional jobs that were available to Blacks were teachers, ministers and barbers. We had some of the best teachers in the county but the subjects covered in our schools were the basics. Music and art were subjects I pursued after leaving there. I learned to swim in recent years. Most of us moved on to obtain professional jobs. When integration of the school did occur, many of our teachers became Chairman of the Department. Yet the relationships formed as kids still are strong and meaningful.

When a group of Ku Klux Klansmen organized a march through the town in recent years, the townsfolk were against it. They could not prevent them from getting a permit to march, so the march took place. What they did do was schedule a rally at the park at a later time inviting all of the townspeople to show unity with a celebration having speakers throughout the community share what the community meant to them. My Aunt Sadie was a major speaker.

I live diversity because I have learned from early on that there are very few things that need separate us and there are many things that we can share to build an even richer community.'

B 'The idea of diversity among people came to me early in life, when as a teen during the 1940s, I began to believe that I was in some way different from my peers. I felt estranged from them, and I experienced feelings of negative self-worth as I discovered that it was socially unacceptable for me to act on the natural feelings within my being.

Later as a college student, I began to conclude that I was a gay man; however, in those days, such a person was advised to 'get over it', or somehow to get a 'cure'. Much of the current thinking encouraged me to find a good woman, marry her, and settle into a 'normal' marriage and family life; somehow the 'unnatural' feelings would then disappear, and life would unfold in the socially-acceptable, normal manner.

Several years after college, I married, and made a commitment to myself and to my wife that I would stay married. This marriage has lasted more than 40 years, has offered both of us many riches from a deep and exciting relationship, has produced two now-grown children, and on the surface is a normal American marriage. My secret, however, is that I didn't 'get over it', or get a 'cure'. I continue to be clearly aware that I am a gay man who has masqueraded as a straight man throughout most of the important activities of my life, including graduate school, and a profession as a college professor.

Life was not that smooth, however. Before I was married, I was 'found out' and fired from my first professional job out of college, for reasons having nothing to do with my professional work. Later, in my work as a personnel manager, I was refused a security clearance by the U.S. Air Force, where my 'secret' again was discovered, and I was subsequently terminated from that position. Still later, after graduate school, I was not granted tenure in an important position as a faculty member of a well-known university – the place for a universe of thought to flourish. It was clear to me that I had been 'out' to too many people at that university. Still another university attempted to fire me, and a federal judge ordered the university to reinstate me. I left that university, for the climate was extremely oppressive with homophobia among the administrators.

For the last 13 years, I have mentioned nothing about my sexual orientation at the Catholic college where I teach, and have been given outstanding praise for the work I have done. It appears that hiding one's self pays off in our society. I am among a fortunate few, for many others of 'difference' cannot hide who they are, for their identity as members of targeted groups is obvious merely by looking at their physical features.

I know about discrimination. I know about difference. I know about oppression, and living a life in hiding. I know about the negative consequences that can arise out of authentically declaring the truth about self.

With the understanding of my own personal experience, I became interested in others who may have experienced 'difference' from the American norm of white, heterosexual, middle-class, male place of privilege. Such people might include persons of African or Hispanic heritages, Native American heritage, women, people who are poor and lacking in education, those who are homosexual, aging, or those disenfranchised by physical or mental disability. After discussing some of these issues with my colleagues, I decided to join them in organizing and facilitating a workshop in diversity – an opportunity for encouraging persons from these diverse backgrounds to come together to share in their experiences coping with 'difference'. And so our first annual workshop entitled 'Experiencing Diversity' was born in 1994. These same colleagues and I have continued in our diversity work since that date, having facilitated four such workshops, with planning underway for our fifth one in October of 1998. These workshops are organized around a person-centered way of being, espoused and researched by the late Carl R. Rogers.'

C 'My neighborhood was pretty homogeneous. There were two principal populations, Italian and Irish, reflecting the city. Even over time we were homogeneous. I played a lot of ball games as my father had before me in the same neighborhood. My ancestors were largely English and Irish, with a little Dutch. Although my family was of moderate income I had the privilege of attending a private school. I never doubted that both of my parents loved and supported me.

It was not till I was college age that I was aware of differences. And I embraced them. I was a unifier. I wanted to unite Math and Poetry, Science and Humanities.

I'm a little more relaxed about these distinctions now. The differences I was interested in were academic, cultural. The cultural differences had to be exotic. I conceived the grand scheme of uniting or finding what was common in China, Japan, India, Islam, and the West.

In later years I got to visit these cultures. I would complete a computer contract and take off. The scheme remained unrealized, but it was a good dream that led to my learning a lot and having many wonderful experiences.

But the local seemed banal, to lack the excitement of the exotic, and all those years I had little to do with the richness and diversity right around me.'

D'I feel that I contributed to the diversity within the facilitating staff by my age and by my limitation of legal blindness which for me means two percent vision in each eye. I grew up in an environment that was not aware of minority groups. However, as I have been thinking about it just now, my hometown had a mix of North Europeans, which included a large Swedish population and a smaller Italian population. I never met a person of color until I went to New York City as an adult, except for two African-American women who made presentations as guests of missionaries. Most of my best friends were Swedish and I realized that there was a class differentiation. The Italians were largely craftsmen, gardeners and nonprofessionals. I was definitely limited in my view of the world!

As I work more intensively with groups, including our facilitating staff, I have learned that I am in another kind of minority. My family was poor. My father drank too much. We moved eight times in my first 16 years. Technically I was an only child, but despite our poverty our house was open to relatives and friends who needed a haven in times of hardship. When, at the age of six, we moved to a farm I had time, with my mother's encouragement, to make friends with nature. Both parents, from my earliest recollection, reassured me of their love and caring for me. It saddens me greatly to find that very few people whom I know have received this kind of reassurance from both parents. In that respect I have discovered that I am part of another kind of minority.

The church-related college which I attended presented only two occasions to meet a person of African descent. They were invited as guests of missionaries. I did well enough academically, became a student assistant to the Professor of English Language and Literature and participated in many extra-curricular activities. I was one of four members of our class who were warned they would be dismissed if we persisted in being 'too liberal in our reading'. Two of the four were dismissed. I was one of the two reprimanded and warned by the administration. My mother offered to help me find another college in case of my dismissal and supported me in standing for what I believed.

I did graduate work at Columbia Teachers College and met and married there the wonderful man with whom I spent 49 years of married life, which ended with his death in 1989. Last year our daughter Mei Mei received her doctorate in anthropology and religion.'

E 'I emigrated to the US when I was seven years old from Scotland. I have early thoughts of being different from the children at my school because I was not American. My parents spoke with accents. My name is a foreign one, so many people mispronounced it. I feel that this set me apart from others.

By the time I reached high school I knew I was gay. I was having a relationship at this time with someone 20 years older than myself. I did not tell anyone about this because I knew I would have to face discriminatory remarks.

I felt separate. I feel that my parents knew I was gay but did not speak to me about it. There was a young Black woman that I ate lunch with everyday. Many students called her nigger and I was the gay nigger lover. I did not think I was different, I knew I was different.

I went to college and was openly gay. I took my chances on being proud of who and what I was. I tried to commit suicide, junior year, because I could not endure the taunts. I came home for a semester and then went back the next year to graduate. Gay or not(!!) I graduated with a BA in sociology. After graduation I did 'come out' to my parents and they asked me to leave the house. I did so, ending up in Syracuse, NY where I met my second lover. We moved to Indiana and spent seven years there. At this time I was drinking heavily; no wonder he left me. I was in the battle of self-medicating myself.

My father died suddenly and I moved back to NY where my drinking escalated. During this time I made 3 attempts on my life and thought that suicide was the only route for a person like me to take. I was not aware that I had a choice to live. I was destined to die, alone, scared, and isolated.

At this time I hooked up with a person-centered therapist who took me to hospital after hospital for more intensive treatment for alcoholism. This person, for the first time, listened to me, listened to my concerns and what a shambles my life was truly in. At one point I called and said, 'This time, I'm really going to do it. There's nothing anyone can do. I called to say goodbye.' At this point the therapist's reply was, 'If you go ahead and end your life, I shall be very sad. I care for you and I'll miss you. But it's your life. You have the right to do whatever you choose with it. And I'll not think the less of you.' I hung up. The next morning I called and said, 'I decided that if someone trusted me that much, I must have something in me worth living for.'

After three years of searching, I was put on lithium and diagnosed manic-depressive. I really did not know what that meant. But I stayed on my medication and went to this helpful therapist for therapy, also becoming a member of a group.

Going on lithium, talking to a person-centered therapist and trying to face what my problems really were, rather than having someone tell me what my problems were, saved my life. And I am able to write this today. I was free in therapy to express my feelings about any topic that I wanted, not what the therapist wanted. This was very new for me. I had to make up my own mind about a lot of things. No one had ever listened to me before and the idea that they listened to me and that I made the choices about what was going to happen was an exceptional experience. It was nothing short of miraculous!! I started to trust myself and the decisions I had made for myself. I started to have patience with myself, instead of throwing in the towel. I learned if there was one way I could not solve a problem, perhaps there was another way I could solve it. I had support, for the first time in my life – *I had support.*

I stopped drinking and came to realize I was an alcoholic. I have not had a drink in 18 years now. I then met my present partner and we have been together for 18 years, having built a life on trust and understanding. I have spent most of the work time in rehabilitative work with Latinos. I am Spanish-speaking and I listened to what their concerns were.

At present I am going to graduate school full-time to become a patient advocate. I am earning a Master's degree in Medical Humanities.

I have spent the better half of my life listening to myself and others because a person-centered therapist took the time to listen to me.

I have been involved with the 'Experiencing Diversity' work for about five years. I have such respect for this work and the people who do this type of work. During this time I have wrestled with cancer, and Parkinson's disease. I have had the support of my person-centered family to help me through the rough times. My friends on the Diversity staff have been invaluable, not in just giving me strength and courage, but I know they will listen to me.

These experiences I bring to the Diversity Staff and hope that my diversity will touch someone else in a good way. I feel I am alive because of this work and I have no shame as to my sexual preference. I am open about that too and prefer to live my life this way. I like the idea that I am accepted for what I am, not for what I am not.

The Diversity staff has allowed me to explore myself and others and their Diversity. It enables me to find out what there is about myself I can improve on and maybe help someone help me when I do not understand their Diversity.

The chance to have a place to express differences and try and explore these differences in a non-threatening way has made all the difference in my life. It has allowed me to create a climate where others can find ways to change their lives.'

F'As far back as I can remember [my family history] all my grandparents were born in Spain, two from Galicia and the others from Las Islas Canarias. My grandmother met my grandfather (mother's side) in Cuba where she was brought to 'save her reputation', as a married man was courting her back home. She never saw her mother or 14 brothers and sisters again. Her father sailed to do business in Cuba once a year where he took her.

My dad's family made it to Cuba via Mexico and he was the 21st child conceived by my grandparents. My mother grew up in poverty, of which she is ashamed, and determined not to be poor, excelled in school. She worked at a private school to help pay for tuition and finally, ten days before leaving Cuba to go to the United States, got her Doctoral degree in Physics and Math – not common for her time, given that she became a single mother at 33 when my father died. I was born in Cuba somewhere in these five years before we left our Island. I grew up in Miami,

Florida where I lived with my mother and brother for a couple of years until we were able to get my grandmother and aunt out of Cuba. I remember my mother being concerned about people not renting to us because we were Cubans, or worse yet, because she had children.

But while a part of me has completely 'assimilated' the 'American Culture', the melting-pot culture, another part of me is as Cuban as they come. I feel I have benefited tremendously from growing up with both cultures where I can choose the best of both worlds. I am now a 43-year-old woman who acknowledged I was a lesbian in my early twenties and have survived my own homophobia. After almost entering the convent in the fall of 1975 I attended and graduated from Florida State University. I have worked in human services for over 20 years. I have also been deeply affected and inspired by the many persons with disabilities that have touched my life during my 25 years plus of professional work. In 1993 I moved to New Britain, Connecticut where I discovered a vibrant though sometimes hostile community. For the first time, while I made a commitment to never forget people with disabilities, I began to work with the 'community' particularly those who are disenfranchised through poverty, language, color, sexuality etc. This town and this work catapulted me into connecting with this wonderful Experiencing Diversity group as I became a citizen of the United States in 1995 and where I purchased a home and ran for City Council in New Britain in 1997. I lost by 200 votes. It was an eye-opening and interesting experience. I believe that people like myself who accept, celebrate and defend diversity need to be sitting at the table where the decisions that affect peoples' lives are made. However, the process of getting there is tainted and difficult to tolerate.'

G 'My name is Maria, but my friends call me Milly. I was born 12-15-78, in Humacao, Puerto Rico, but was raised in Maunabo, Puerto Rico. My mother was born and raised in Maunabo, Puerto Rico in 1952. She is a very religious person, and attends a Pentecostal church. My father also was born and raised in Maunabo, Puerto Rico in 1948.

My father and mother got a divorce when I was six-years-old. The reason they got divorced was because my father is an alcoholic, and every time he drank he became violent.

I enjoyed the time I spent in Puerto Rico. It was beautiful. We lived at my grandmother's house next to the beach. My father used to take my brother Luisito and me, on walks along the beach. I used to love those moments.

When I was seven my mom came to the United States, to fight for custody of my sister, Bernice who came here (U.S.A.) to spend time with relatives of ours. While she was staying here, her father took her to live with him. When my mother realized that it was going to take a while for her to gain custody, she sent for us to come live with her here. Ever since then we have been living in the United States. It was a big change for me because I left behind my father, grandmother, other family and friends and my beautiful Island.

Since I was a little girl I had a hard time going to school. Fourth and fifth grade

I barely went to school. In Junior High School I tried to attend more, but I wasn't successful. Through all that time I went through a lot of emotional problems and depressions. I didn't often leave my house, I didn't want to. The Department of Social Services wanted to take me away from my family because I didn't attend school. It was very scary and depressing. When I finally reached High School I got good help from a counselor named Carla. She helped me a lot. I found out with this counselor that I have some kind of social phobia, which was helpful to know. Because of Carla I met a lot of wonderful people, that helped me improve my life and she also was the one who invited me to the Diversity Workshops.

Since then a lot of good things have happened to me. I don't have social phobia, I work, I am an Experiencing Diversity staff member, I do volunteer work, my grandmother is living over here (U.S.A.) now, my father has stopped drinking alcohol for a couple of years now, and my brother Luisito and I have gone to visit him in Puerto Rico. I have the *best* mother, I could tell her anything, my brother Luisito is my best friend, my sister could be a pain but a good one, I have four beautiful nephews, I have very *good* friends, and best of all I have God, that always helps me. There is one thing that I am still working on and that is school, I am getting better but not good enough. I want to continue my education because I want to work in the field of social services.'

Summary of learnings from our experiencing diversity workshops
This list of learnings gleaned from the experience identified by one member of the group may be helpful to future planning groups who are interested in planning an 'experiencing diversity' workshop. We hope the learnings of other planning group members, participants, and later workshops will be added to it.

Composition
If we wanted to experience diversity we needed to have a diverse staff. We needed to have time for a diverse staff to come together as a group which valued and appreciated each other. We found we needed not a few weeks but a year to achieve this feeling of oneness.

It was important that we try to apply the person-centered approach in our own thinking, in our own way and ways of being together, rather than trying to do a workshop that taught about the person-centered approach. One member of the planning group said he had experienced a sense of belonging for which he had been longing all his life.

Organization
Personal contacts and personal distribution of materials were more effective than mass mailings. Mailings were more effective if accompanied by a personal letter.

Rather than setting a rockbottom conference fee for those who could pay, it was agreed that it was better for participants to invest a reasonable amount and at the same time recognize the value of the facilitation offered. In order to ensure the availability of scholarships, we have made efforts to raise funds by appealing to prominent members and institutions of the communities in which staff members live, and by writing grant proposals. Thus far we have been able to offer scholarships wherever needed and to provide seed money for the following year. The fee remained substantially lower than most workshops of this nature. All members of the planning group volunteered their services. We needed to put together enough by means of registration, grants, and contributions to provide 'scholarships without a stigma' for those who could not pay the fee. The financial arrangements of each participant were held in confidence. That we did this proved to be a key to the general feeling of belonging that was important to the success of the workshop.

We also discovered that it is important to include as members of the planning group, persons who are in daily contact with groups who we are trying to reach via such organizations as colleges or universities, social service centers working with minority groups, municipal community agencies, rehabilitation programs, gay and lesbian groups, unemployment services, and so forth.

In order to build a genuine sense of community among the planning group, we discovered the need to emphasize from the beginning the importance of commitment, to attend meetings at agreed-upon times over a period of approximately a year. We lost considerable time when members of the group who had been absent at a previous meeting asked to be brought up to date. We also lost time because individual members came late or had to leave early.

The decision not to hold the workshop on a university campus or to be sponsored by a university or religious organization seems in retrospect to have been a wise decision. Some members of minority groups are intimidated, 'put off', by such an association. International House in New York City for us seemed a natural. There was considerable degree of agreement between the purpose of Experiencing Diversity and the mission of International House. From the beginning, International House held out an invitation to international students. It seemed a perfect liaison. In 1996, after two years at International House, we recognized a need to have a conference site that would be wheelchair accessible in order to encourage participants who are physically challenged. We decided on Hemlocks, an Easter Seal Society conference center in Hebron, Connecticut, familiar to three members of the staff from previous conferences. It is located on 160 acres of woodland in rural Connecticut. Many sports facilities are available: a swimming pool, a stage, a cafeteria, and large comfortable meeting rooms with fireplaces, and windows looking out over the lake.

The selection of a meeting place presents a problem, the solution of which depends on each unique situation. A large metropolitan site can be intimidating and distracting to some potential participants, but at the same time is close to large numbers of minority groups for whom the workshop is designed.

We worked very closely from the beginning with those responsible for making facilities available to groups such as ours. Understanding of our objectives by International House staff engendered acceptance, warmth and flexibility, all of which contributed to creating a climate in which the workshop could flourish.

We recognized the importance of providing adequate transportation facilities. One of the major factors in selecting a place for the group is the availability of transportation to participants at low or no cost to wherever needed.

After considerable discussion, we decided to use a meeting place of easy access by public transportation. Transportation problems were minimized by the offer of members of the planning group from Pennsylvania, Massachusetts and Connecticut to bring their groups by van or car. We made sure parking facilities nearby were available.

We also made sure inexpensive housing or living arrangements in or near the place of meeting were available: International House, International-House Annex, a hostel, and rooms in private homes.

Scheduling
We needed a weekend that extended into a fourth day to allow time for evaluation and planning for the facilitating staff. This also helped people who had come a long way. They could stay over an additional night, have breakfast, and an additional day to return to their homes. There is an advantage to establishing a given weekend of the year as the usual time for holding the annual workshop. A legal holiday weekend such as Columbus Day makes extension to the following Monday possible.

Esprit de corps
I would like to underscore the importance of developing a relationship of trust among members of the facilitating staff so that they can take care of their own personal needs within that community rather than carrying them over to the workshops. Then the facilitative staff is freed to enter the workshop as facilitative participants.

Through our struggle together to find our way in unknown territory, we came to know one another in a wide range of experiencing, to be real and open, to accept, to trust, to appreciate each other as we were, in moments of stress as well as exhilaration, to care more deeply about each other – to become as one in our feeling of community. It was this spirit, this sense of community, that seemed to be 'caught' by the participants in the workshop.

A look to the future
I recall a beautiful Chinese calligraphy that has a special place on my living-room wall, 'Within the four seas, all men are brothers'. It was written by a dear Chinese friend, calligrapher for the Library of Congress and Chinese Diplomat. Translating it into less poetic wording, we could say, 'Within the world in which we live, we are all members of the human family'. I ask myself the question, from our own small communities around the world, 'Are we moving to realization of the hope expressed in ancient China?'

I do not recall that my parents quarreled or fought, but I am sure that I grew up aware of their sharp differences, and I must have felt safe because I was not frightened nor am I frightened now of such interchanges. I may find them very painful but my tendency is to see what I can learn from it and what I can do about it. In my opinion this tendency did not just happen but was nourished by the realities of my family life in my early years. Perhaps we with our differences within the extended PCA families as they reach out in many parts of the world may do something similar. I am sure I am not alone in this discovery, and I am sure we have not found the only way. The PCA is the way I know best and therefore trust. I am open to find other ways as well.

References

Sanford, R. (1987) An Inquiry into the Evolution of the Client-Centered Approach to Psychotherapy. in Zeig, J. (ed), *The Evolution of Psychotherapy*. New York: Brunner/Mazel.

RESEARCH

Client-centred Psychotherapy in Groups: Understanding the Influence of the Client-Therapist Relationship on Therapy Outcome

6

Peter Figge

It seems that client-centred psychotherapy (CCP) is out of fashion. This concept of psychotherapy centring around the attitude of supporting the inner resources of people in personal need by acceptance and understanding seems to appear too simple in the recent psychotherapeutic environment. Elaborate theories, glittering multi-media approaches in problem solving, and dramatic intervention techniques head the popularity lists, promising patients, insurance companies and social security systems highest cost/output ratios in the shortest time possible. Sometimes not being regarded as a form of psychotherapy of its own, client-centred psychotherapy is considered as a mere technique of relating to clients, elements of this technique being worthwhile to integrate into various other forms of psychotherapy.

One has to recall, however, that CCP has a long standing not merely as a technique of psychotherapeutic relationship. CCP with its specific theoretical background (Rogers, 1973, 1987; Lietaer et al., 1990; Grawe et al., 1994) can look back on a well-founded tradition of successful practice and widely published research. When clinical criteria are applied CCP has proven to be a most effective form of psychotherapy supporting the process of internal growth in clients. By furthering self-acceptance and self understanding CCP meets the needs of clients to be unconditionally understood. Empathy offered by client-centred psychotherapists enables patients to be increasingly empathetic and acceptant towards themselves in order to gain personal development, to cope with crises in life, and to solve problems while integrating the understanding of their own emotional, cognitive and behavioural experiences.

Thus it is not by chance that a recent study (Figge et al., 1994) revealed that CCP is the form of psychotherapy most widely spread and most frequently used at counselling centres of German institutions of higher education. CCP is being applied in more than two-thirds of the counselling institutions which offer psychological counselling and psychotherapy for students. In 36 % of the cases client-centred psychotherapy is being used, followed by psychoanalytic methods (17 %), and behaviour therapy (16 %).

It is in view of this discrepancy – the ambivalent status of CCP as a seemingly unfashionable approach on one hand and the actual degree of wide application within for example the academic environment on the other hand – that some results of a study (Figge & Schwab, 1997) on the effects of CCP are reported. This study comprises a process of nearly ten years of client-centred psychotherapy in groups with students. It accentuates the degree of effectiveness of CCP as well as it points out certain process factors regarding the differential ways in which this psychotherapeutic approach works.

A study on client-centred psychotherapy in groups

Fifty-eight students (32 f, 26 m; age mean: 27.9 years) of Hamburg University and associated institutions of higher education who sought psychotherapeutic help at the Counselling and Psychotherapy Centre of Hamburg University participated in a one-year client-centred group-psychotherapy. Seven students did not finish the therapy due to various reasons.

The problems mainly presented correspond to the following diagnostic categories according to ICD-10 (World Health Organization 1991): F31 – Bipolar affective disorder, F32 – Depressive episode, F34 – Cyclothymia, F40 – Phobic anxiety disorders, F41 – Other anxiety disorders, F43 – Acute stress reaction, F50 – Eating disorders, F51 – Non-organic sleep disorder, F52 – Sexual disfunction, and F60 – Specific personality disorders.

After four single diagnostic sessions, CCP consisted of two-hour group sessions once a week for a period of one year, including a one-day and a three-day 'intensive session' in the seclusion of a country meeting place. A therapy group consisted of a maximum of eight clients (male and female) one female junior, and one male senior psychotherapist.

Criteria for the consideration of group therapy did not centre around specific symptoms and problems. The four initial interviews served diagnostic and indicative purposes: to understand a state of incongruence in the clients resulting from not being able to fully integrate personal experiences into the individual self; to estimate the client's ability to positively react to the therapist's CCP attitudes: empathy, unconditional regard and congruence; to judge the clients' ability to relate to the therapists and the readiness to welcome this form of psychotherapy as a potential agent for personal change.

CCP aims to offer certain conditions to the client in which s/he will feel understood and unconditionally accepted by congruent others within a therapy setting, no more but also no less. Ideally psychotherapy will be over when the client has conceded to treat himself or herself with the same attitudes of empathy, unconditional regard and congruence which s/he has experienced from the therapists and other group members.

Clients who will profit from CCP do not look for theoretical explanations of their problems, they definitely abhor goal-oriented behaviour-therapy perspectives as well as any dependence on therapists in emotion-inducing therapeutic approaches. Extensive meta-studies by Grawe et al (1990a,b, 1994) on the differential effectiveness of psychotherapeutic approaches point out that clients with a special need for autonomy and self-determination and a high resistance to therapeutic directiveness will in comparison profit most from an approach like CCP. This differentiation supports the findings of studies by Beutler et al., (1991), Hoogduin et al., (1989), Quintana et al., (1990) and Talley et al., (1990) which underline the importance of the individually matched therapeutic relationship on the potential outcome of therapy.

In this study extensive data (based on personality questionnaires, ratings and interviews) was collected before and after the psychotherapy as well as six months after the last group-psychotherapy session. Some of the results obtained are exemplarily reported below and give indications regarding the differential effectiveness and characteristics of the therapy process in client-centred group-psychotherapy with students (Figge & Schwab, 1997).

Therapy–outcome
The form of client-centred group-psychotherapy investigated in this study is effective. In accordance with published data regarding the effectiveness of client-centred psychotherapy (for an overview see Grawe et al., 1994), significant positive development can be observed within the 37 variables measured in different personality questionnaires (see Table 1, column 1).

The effects of client-centred psychotherapy in groups can be observed on the intersubjective level regarding the self-concept (depressiveness, emotional lability, composure, nervousness) as well as on the interpersonal level regarding the symbolisation of one's own capability to relate to others (sociability, inhibition, social potency). When the therapy is effective the individual self-concept is examined and newly defined within the process of therapy. In consequence, the self-concept approaches the ideal-self.

Client development gained through client-centred group-psychotherapy does not only lead to a modified generalized assessment of the self but also to new manifestations of behaviour in real life situations.

Consistent with the assumptions of CCP, individual change related to therapy is for example reflected in a decrease of a prior state of individual incongruence. Incongruence being understood as a state of developmental stagnation on cognitive, emotional and behavioural levels which prohibits the integration of experience within the self-concept (Biermann-Ratjen et al., 1995; Biermann-Ratjen & Swildens, 1993). In the process of a client-centred psychotherapy this integration will be made possible. Within CCP the experiences of the client will be subject to a re-evaluation, they will be symbolised in a different way and thus change their significance. This process contributes to a modification of the self-concept which together with the newly acquired capability to integrate and symbolise experiences will constitute the onset of the desired process of developmental growth.

Early research (Butler and Haigh, 1954) on CCP had already suggested that

Variable	Mean differences pre – post (outcome)	Correlations outcome with therapist-dimensions				
		Empathy	Active engagement	Congruence	Positive regard	Social power
Giessen-Test (self-concept)						
Social resonance	+**			**		
Dominance						
Internal control				*		
Depressiveness	–***			*		
Retention	–**					
Social potency						
Giessen-Test (ideal-self)						
Social resonance		*	*	**		
Dominance						
Internal control			*			*
Depressiveness						
Retention						
Social potency						
Discrepancy (abs.values) GT (self-concept/ideal-self)						
Social resonance				**		
Dominance						
Internal control	–**					
Depressiveness	–**					
Retention				*		
Social potency	–***					

Freiburg Personality Inventory					
Nervousness	–***				
Aggressiveness					
Depressiveness	–***	**	**	**	*
Excitability	+**		**		
Sociability	+		*		
Composure	+				
Dominance					
Inhibition	–***				
Frankness					
Extraversion		*	***		
Emotional lability	–*	*	***		
Masculinity	+***	*	*		
Insecurity and Anxiety Questionnaire					
General anxiety	–***		*	*	
Criticism and failure	–***	*	*	**	*
Inability to say no	–***				
Shyness in social interaction	–***		*	**	
Inability to demand	–***				
Feelings of guilt in social interaction	–**			*	
Extensive politeness	–***				

Table 1. List of significant results (N=51):
1. Change pre/post testing: + signifying an increase of variable, – signifying a decrease of variable values (*=p.05, **=p.01, ***=p.001).
2. Correlations: outcome/therapist dimensions (*=p.05, **=p.01, ***=p.001).

for example extensive discrepancies between individual concepts of the self and the contrasting ideal self may constitute a source of incongruence which motivates people to seek psychotherapeutic help.

Correspondingly positive therapy outcome in this study is associated with a significant decrease in the self/ideal-self dimension, reducing significantly the discrepancy of 'how I see myself' and 'how I want to be' to a manageable and healthy tension between the experience of the self and the aspirations and hopes embedded in a potential ideal self (see Table 1).

Taken from group data, Figure 1 and Figure 2 illustrate this process of therapy-induced change in an individual client. Figure 1 describes data on the self/ideal self-perception of this client gathered at the first testing. Apart from noting a self-concept that can be characterised as highly depressive and retentive as well as by very low social resonance and potency, a large discrepancy between self and ideal self can be observed in some of the variables. At the end of therapy (Figure 2) this discrepancy has not only been remarkably decreased, but marked changes can also be observed regarding self as well as ideal self-concepts within the different dimensions.

The therapeutic relationship

The quality of client-therapist relationship was very early postulated by CCP (Rogers, 1987, 1988, 1991) to be one of the major factors responsible for therapeutic change.

Instead of judging, however, the therapist's behaviour by exterior raters according to CCP concept variables as has been the custom in the past – (Barrett-Lennard, 1962), the main interest in this study centred around the clients' subjective experience of their therapist. As the author had been the senior therapist in all therapy groups included in this study, differences in the way the clients experienced the relationship to this therapist might shed a light on the influence of client/therapist relationship on therapy outcome.

The instrument used in this study to evaluate the quality of the client-therapist relationship was the 'Questionnaire of therapeutic relationship' (Figge, 1980), a 37-item questionnaire answered by the clients at the end of their group therapy. Factor analysis of this questionnaire with clients in client-centred psychotherapy has revealed five dimensions according to which the psychotherapist is perceived. Figure 3 lists the dimensions of perception along with examples of items. Illustrations selected by clients to clarify the associative content of these dimensions are added to illustrate the corresponding experience.

The dimensions of experience describe the three classical attitudes of CC psychotherapists towards their clients: empathy, unconditional regard and congruence. Additionally concepts of engagement and social power form part of the clients' perception. It may be noted that this form of experience is unique to a client-centred setting since different dimensions of client/therapist relationship were revealed when the same therapist was perceived in a behaviour therapy group setting (Figge, 1980, 1982).

Table 1 indicates that therapeutic change (outcome) as measured by

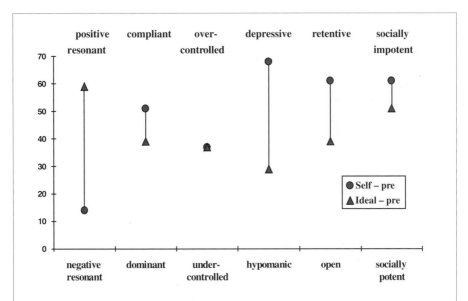

Figure 1.   Case study GT 97
Gießen-Test. Self and Ideal-Self (Pre-Testing)

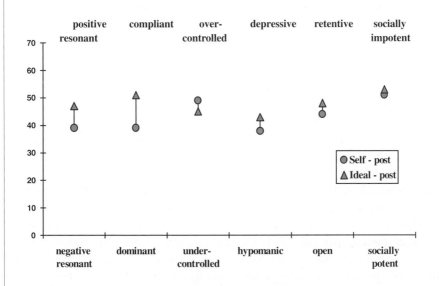

Figure 2.   Case study GT 97
Gießen-Test. Self and Ideal-Self (Post-Testing)

Figure 3.   Dimensions of the 'Questionnaire of therapeutic relationship'
(Figge, 1980)   Examples of items

1. Empathy (9 items)

- He understands me.
- He is interested in finding out what my experience means to me.
- He often knows what I mean, even when I have difficulty expressing it.

2. Active engagement (7 items)

- It seems to me that he is not committed in his efforts.
- He is generally lacking in energy and enthusiasm.
- I sometimes have the impression that he should make more effort.

3. Congruence (8 items)

- I feel that he plays a role with me.
- I feel that he is completely genuine and honest towards me.
- Sometimes I feel that the things he says to me are completely different from what he feels inside.

4. Positive regard (8 items)

- He respects me as a person.
- He is really interested in me.
- If I show that I am annoyed with him, he becomes annoyed with me as well or is hurt.

5. Social power (5 items)

- I wish I were like him.
- It means a lot to me when he praises me.
- It is good for me when I follow his instructions.

questionnaires is related to certain attitudes of the psychotherapist as experienced by the client. Whereas the amount of social power perceived seems not to be important to individual profit from therapy, the experience of the therapist as being congruent may be considered to play a major role in the developmental process. As might be predicted a significant influence of empathy, positive regard and engagement on therapy outcome can also be observed.

An analysis of variance comparing groups of clients with different degrees of therapeutic success made a further differentiation possible. Apparently clients experienced the same therapist in different ways. Evaluating the significance of these perceptions, it seems that the main variables to further positive outcome in CCP can be identified as empathy and congruence. Mainly those clients who observed the therapist as being highly congruent and empathetic towards themselves profited most from this form of group psychotherapy. Further research (Figge & Schwab, 1997) on the development of the client-therapist relationship during the course of therapy indicates that the clients' experience of congruence of the therapist (i.e., the perception of genuineness, honesty and reliability) may be a precondition on which the offer of empathy is being accepted and therapeutically used by the client.

It should be pointed out again, however that empathy, congruence, positive regard and engagement were not seen here as elements of therapist behaviour as observed from the outside. Only if these were identified as reliable attitudes of the therapist by the individual client while primarily experiencing the therapist as being congruent – do these therapist dimensions fully unsheathe their therapeutic qualities.

The concept of congruence which has been defined by Rogers (1987, 1988) as 'Genuineness/Congruence/Realness' has always been subject to contradictory interpretations. On one hand this concept was understood to suggest a maximum amount of self-disclosure of the therapist towards the client, modelling an openness towards one's own feelings and avoiding any client/therapist hierarchy within the therapeutic setting.

On the other hand and in the sense it is used here – congruence is understood as the therapist's process gaining access to his/her own feelings and being open to the process of its adequate symbolisation and integration – in order to be able to understand the client empathetically (Biermann-Ratjen et al., 1995). The therapist therefore does not set out to share his/her own feelings with the client or to confront him/her with the therapist's inner state, but aspires to be able to experience the world of the client by not being preoccupied or hindered by his or her own feelings.

A congruent therapist is valued by clients as an important other who understands and accepts the client's experiences from the client's viewpoint being aware of their different status in the relationship. Thus the promise of a congruent CC therapist consists in attempting to understand his/her own feelings in the therapeutic setting in order to be able to offer unhindered empathy to the client.

Congruence is the precondition for empathy. Empathy is here defined as the attitude of the therapist which gives words to the subjective inner frame of reference of the client, and which thus offers acceptance to the individual significance of the client's experience. Empathy by the therapist allows the client to adequately symbolise his/her experiences through self empathy. Being able to integrate these experiences into their own self concept, the client's state of incongruence is dissolved.

Conclusion

The results of this study support recent findings and assumptions that positive therapy effects are largely dependent on a special approachability of the individual client towards a given method of psychotherapy and towards the respective psychotherapist. CCP is a successful form of psychotherapy in which a therapist offers a very special form of relationship. Clients who are able to accept this relationship as supportive, are sensitive in distinguishing the helpful attitudes of the therapist which are offered to them. Empathy which has long been known as a central agent of therapeutic change is reliant on the precondition of therapist congruence to fully become effective.

References

Barrett-Lennard, G.T. (1962). Dimensions of therapist response as causal factors in therapeutic change. *Psychol. Monographs*. Whole Nr. 562

Beutler, L.E., Engle, D., Mohr, D., Daldrup, R.J., Bergan, J., Meredith, K. & Merry, W. (1991). Predictors of differential response to cognitive, experiential, and self-directed psychotherapeutic procedures. *Journal of Consulting and Clinical Psychology, 59,* 333–340.

Biermann-Ratjen, E., Eckert, J. & Schwartz, H.J. (1995). *Gesprächspsychotherapie.* (7. Aufl.). Stuttgart: Kohlhammer .

Biermann-Ratjen, E.M. & Swildens, H. (1993). Entwurf einer ätiologisch orientierten Krankheitslehre im Rahmen des klientenzentrierten Konzeptes. In: J. Eckert, D. Höger, & H. Linster, (Hrsg.), *Die Entwicklung der Person und ihre Störung*. Köln: GwG-Verlag, 57– 42.

Butler, J.M., Haigh, G.V. (1954). Changes in the Relation between Self-Concepts and Ideal Concepts Consequent upon Client-Centred Counseling. In: Rogers, C.R., Dymond, R.F., Eds., *Psychotherapy and Personality Change*. Chicago.

Figge, P. (1980). *Dramatherapie bei Studenten mit Kontaktstörungen*. Dissertation Universität Hamburg, Fachbereich Psychologie.

Figge, P. (1982). *Dramatherapie bei Kontaktstörungen: Spielräume erlebensbezogener Verhaltenstherapie*. München: Kösel.

Figge, P., Kaiphas, W., Knigge-Illner, H. and Rott, G. (1994). Germany – Psychological Counselling in Higher Education. In: E. Bell, C. McDevitt, G. Rott & P. Valerio (Hrsg.), *Psychological Counselling in Higher Education. A European Overview (*S. 39–66).Neapel, Istituto Italiana per gli Studi Filosofici.

Figge, P. & Schwab, R. (1997). Klientenzentrierte Psychotherapie in Gruppen. Objektiver und subjektiver Therapieerfolg unter dem Einfluß der erlebten Beziehung zum Therapeuten. *Gesprächspsychotherapie und Personzentrierte*

Beratung 1, 22–36.

Grawe, K., Caspar, F. & Ambühl, H. (1990a). Die Berner Therapie-Vergleichsstudie: Wirkungsvergleich und differentielle Indikation. *Zeitschrift für Klinische Psychologie, 19,* 338–361.

Grawe, K., Caspar, F. & Ambühl, H. (1990b). Die Berner Therapie-Vergleichsstudie: Zusammenfassung und Schlußfolgerungen. *Zeitschrift für Klinische Psychologie, 19,* 362–376.

Grawe, K., Donati, R.& Bernauer, F. (1994). *Psychotherapie im Wandel. Von der Konfession zur Profession.* Göttingen: Hogrefe.

Hoogduin, C.A.L., de Haan, E. & Schaap, C. (1989). The significance of the patient-therapist relationship in the treatment of obsessive-compulsive neurosis. *British Journal of Clinical Psychology, 28,* 185–186.

Lietaer,G., Rombauts, J., van Balen, R. (Eds.) (1990). *Client-centered and experiential psychotherapy.* Leuven: Leuven University Press.

Quintana, S.M. & Meara, N.M. (1990). Internalization of therapeutic relationships in short-term psychotherapy. *Journal of Counseling Psychology, 37,* 123–130.

Rogers, C.R. (1973). *Die klient-bezogene Gesprächstherapie.* München: Kindler. (Original: *Client-centered Therapy.* Boston: Houghton Mifflin, 1951).

Rogers, C.R. (1987). Eine Theorie der Psychotherapie, der Persönlichkeit und der zwischenmenschlichen Beziehungen. Entwickelt im Rahmen des klientenzentrierten Ansatzes. Köln: GwG. (Original: A theory of therapy, personality and interpersonal relationships as developed in the client-centered framework. In: S. Koch (Ed.), *Psychology: A study of a science.* New York: McGraw-Hill, 1959).

Rogers, C.R. (1988). *Therapeut und Klient* (4. Aufl.). Frankfurt/M: Fischer. 211–230 (Original (1962): The interpersonal relationship: the core of guidance. *Harvard Educational Review*, 42, 416–429)

Rogers, C.R. (1991). Die notwendigen und hinreichenden Bedingungen für Persönlichkeitsentwicklung durch Psychotherapie. In: C.R. Rogers & P.F. Schmid, *Person-zentriert. Grundlagen von Theorie und Praxis.* S. 165–184. Mainz: Matthias-Grünewald. (Original (1957): The necessary and sufficient conditions of therapeutic personality change. *Journal of Consulting Psychology, 21,* 95–103).

Talley, P.F., Strupp, H.H. & Morey, L.C. (1990). Matchmaking in psychotherapy: Patient-therapist dimensions and their impact on outcome. *Journal of Consulting and Clinical Psychology, 58,* 182–188.

World Health Organization (1991). *Tenth Revision of the International Classification of Diseases, Chapter V (F): Mental and Behavioural Disorders (including disorders of psychological development).* Clinical Descriptions and Diagnostic Guidelines. World Health Organization: Geneva 1991.

APPLICATIONS

A Person-Centred Approach to the Facilitation of Citizens' Juries: A Recent Development in Public Consultation

7

Jane Hoffman

Twenty-one empty chairs sit in a circle. A table holds coffee and tea. The room is silent. I check the clock again – twenty-five minutes to go. I feel my heart beating – have we remembered everything? What if nobody turns up – God, I need a fag[1]! Why did I ever get involved in this? I could be snuggled up at home right now waiting for Coronation Street[2] to start. Instead, here I am in a bare, unfamiliar Community Centre, with butterflies doing cartwheels in my stomach, on the brink of an experience that, at this moment, is a terrifying and exciting unknown.

Such were my thoughts one evening in early 1997 as, with two colleagues, I waited for the members of the first Scottish Citizens' Jury to arrive.

Kate, Hugh and I, at time of writing, have now worked with three Citizens' Juries in Scotland. What follows is a personal reflection of my learning from the experiences and the philosophy that underpins this method of public consultation which fits with my own person-centred belief system.

What is a citizens' jury?
Citizens' Juries, as they have become known in the UK, draw on the experience of work undertaken in the United States, Germany and other European countries over the past twenty years. Introduced to Britain in 1996 by The Institute for Public Policy Research, the approach has been developed by them with Opinion Leader Research (Coote and Lenaghan 1997). Since then juries have been commissioned by a range of public bodies including local authorities and health boards to explore contentious public issues for which there are no simple or straightforward solutions.

---

[1] British slang for a cigarette
[2] A popular British TV soap opera

The basic features of a Citizens' Jury are:
- An issue is identified as of major concern to a particular population.
- 16–20 'jurors' are recruited using standard market research techniques to be representative of that population in terms of age, gender, working status, etc.
- The jury meets to explore the issue over a period of several full days following an Introductory session.
- Jurors question and take evidence from 'witnesses' – people who have particular expertise in, or direct experience of the issue under consideration.
- Jurors can meet in both plenary and small group sessions for discussion.
- At the end of the process, the jury puts forward a series of recommendations to the commissioning body as to how they feel the issue can be tackled.
- The commissioning body contract with the jurors to implement as many of their recommendations as possible and to explain why others cannot be implemented.
- The jurors receive a fee and expenses.
- The process is facilitated, from recruitment through to completion of a written report, by independent facilitators to ensure the integrities of both the jury and the commissioning body.

For our Scottish juries, each commissioned by a local authority, the recruitment processes screened out community activists, elected councillors, council employees or anyone with a particular 'axe to grind' (vested interest). Ideally, the jury comprises people with a concern for the issue being examined but who hold no position of authority or influence – ordinary members of a particular population.

The belief is that such a group of people, if provided with an appropriate and respectful environment and with time and information, is capable of making constructive recommendations about how their community's problems can be addressed. Thus, solutions to their problems are their own, which echo the person-centred approach I offer in my private counselling practice.

Something new
My excitement was great when Hugh brought home the original brief. Hugh is my husband and a market research consultant with whom I worked as a researcher until twelve years ago when I chose to pursue a different path that led eventually to person-centred counselling training. What I read in that brief, felt like an opportunity to draw together two previously completely separate parts of my working self and experience. Here also was a chance for Hugh and I to work together again.

In the past as a market researcher, I was regularly commissioned to conduct group discussions, now more trendily known as focus groups, among members of the general public. Typically, each group comprised 8–10 respondents who, to my agenda, provided evidence over 60–90 minutes of their existing opinions, attitudes and experience in relation to a particular product, advertising campaign or service. I then analysed and interpreted the information I had gathered from respondents and drew *my* conclusions and made *my* recommendations to assist my client with marketing decisions.

In direct contrast, the final recommendations of each Citizens' Jury are composed by the jurors themselves and reflect *their* interpretation of an issue and what *they* would like to see happen about it.

My facilitation of a jury, therefore, would be very different to the moderation of a market research focus group. I would not be using the jurors as sources of information for my purposes. Instead, I would be helping to provide the atmosphere, environment and practical assistance to support them as a fact-finding, decision-making group.

And yet, a jury group is like no other group that I have encountered since becoming involved in person-centred counselling/personal development work. A Citizens' Jury is commissioned following a competitive tendering process, the 'client' is the commissioning body, the jury has a very specific task to tackle, is time-limited and makes a formal presentation of its findings.

My various backgrounds in market research and counselling/personal development work were neither, therefore, on their own precisely relevant. Both encouraged me, however, to believe that it would be possible to adopt a person-centred approach to the facilitation of a task-orientated public consultation exercise.

This belief led me, in our formal proposal for the work, back to basic person-centred principles of empowerment and valuing of each individual within the group, when describing the approach our facilitation would take. In this context, it felt a little like working in the dark. We were not aware at that time of any published material about Citizens' Juries – our previous knowledge was limited to a brief 'Newsnight'[3] report of an English jury which had met to consider a local illegal drugs problem.

In retrospect, I can appreciate the freedom the 'blank slate' afforded, to think the project through from scratch without the distraction of precedent. In the same way, I prefer to have no prior information about a new counselling client.

When, later, we did have sight of a full report on a previous jury, it was a strange and exciting experience. What I read about the facilitative approach adopted there was exactly mirrored in what I had described in our proposal. It felt as if I must have seen this report before, which of course I had not, but the sense of affirmation was huge: my wish to integrate both parts of my working self now seemed really possible.

It was fortunate that our first client, a medium-sized Scottish local authority, understood that the philosophy of empowerment and respect for the individual was not merely jargon but was the rationale that would determine our whole attitude in the design and implementation of the project.

Planning
Having agreed a broad outline for four main jury days, we set about the detailed

---

[3] *A TV current affairs programme*

planning. There were a number of important considerations:

- A group of strangers was going to meet and work together for a prolonged period.
- These people would not have been involved in anything like this before.
- Neither had we! – in fact, Kate (my counsellor colleague), Hugh and myself had not worked together as a team before.
- The group was task-orientated.
- We hoped that the experience could be a good one for the jurors.
- As the first such project in Scotland, we felt a lot of pressure to 'get it right'.

It was vital that the atmosphere surrounding the whole project was both enabling and respectful of everyone involved but without any sense of being patronising. Participants must have the power to influence proceedings (take ownership of the jury). The pacing of the programme should not be too onerous and physical needs should be well catered for.

And yet, at the point of making such arrangements before the first jury, we had no knowledge of the people we were to be working with beyond that they were all resident in one particular geographical area, would include males and females and cover a range of ages and working status.

The Council were generous in their choice of premises, providing comfortable, private surroundings with excellent catering. That the jury should meet in a council-owned venue was something of a compromise over our original thinking which had preferred 'neutral' territory, but in the event I don't believe that the location had any significantly adverse influence on proceedings.

At this stage, I became very aware of my personal shift in attitude to the project. In my market researcher days, I would have been almost totally preoccupied with the logistics of the timings, topics, recording equipment and the like. Now, while still acknowledging the importance of such attention to detail, I found myself largely concentrating on how I could prepare for the forthcoming experience in a way that would be facilitative of the still unknown but potentially disparate needs of the group.

This led me to think hard about how I wanted to 'be' within the group which led in turn to acknowledging conflicting parts of myself. There was the part that wanted to structure towards the completion of the task (my children call this part of me 'bossy') and the part that held a real trust that the group process would do what it needed to do, in its own way.

I am glad I gave attention to my internal struggle as it led me to recognise that jurors too might have to go through similar processes of personal negotiation, not only as individuals but also as members of a group seeking consensus.

One preparation we made as facilitators was to spend time with a colleague exploring our relationships and our hopes and fears around working together as a team. The beauty of hindsight allows me now to recognise those issues we didn't talk about in this meeting – but it seems we had to have the experience to know the real relevance of our different relationships with each other – but more of that later.

The roles that we initially agreed as a team have remained largely constant over all three juries – Hugh offering himself in a chairman/co-ordinator role in order to hold agreed boundaries around, for example, time-keeping and 'one-at-a-time' participation. He remains open at all times to collective or individual needs to change or amend procedures, thus underlining the jurors' ownership of the project.

Kate and I primarily focus on the individual members of the group, using active listening skills to help promote confidence and encourage group interaction. In this, we have become increasingly aware that, although jury members make a considerable commitment when they agree to 'serve' in this way, they have lives outside the jury room which cannot be ignored and sometimes demand attention. I have been moved by the jurors' dedication and determination when dealing with such distractions – even serious domestic and health problems. They have seemed not to want to miss a minute more than was absolutely essential.

The process begins
The moment eventually came before the first jury, however, when no more preparation was possible. Anxious feelings, as described in my opening lines, filled the gap between what seemed like two distinct stages in the project.

First there had been the detailed planning and setting-up stage over which we had control. Then came the Introductory Evening, when the thoughts, words and names previously just marks on pieces of paper, came alive in the shape of human beings. Time for us to relinquish control and trust in group process which would begin its own journey – to wherever.

I tried to deal with my anxiety by first acknowledging that I would be inhuman not to be feeling nervous but also then imagining how each of these men and women might be feeling as they came into the hall, uncertain of what they were letting themselves in for and who else might be there and what was going to happen, etc. Here was my first opportunity to show my valuing of each individual. What did I naturally do? Offer them a smiling face – a cup of tea. Sugar and milk?

The purpose of having an Introductory Evening for each jury was for the group to form in as relaxed a manner as possible with opportunities for everyone to meet each other and find out exactly what was being asked of them. Kate and I offered 'ice-breaking' exercises chosen to introduce twenty-one strangers in a way that would hopefully be non-threatening, but also fun and as much like normal behaviour as possible.

While not wishing to diminish the value of that early work with jurors, I ask myself whether part of the reason why all the groups we have so far worked with seemed to gel very quickly was that the members of each group already shared a common concern – i.e., the topic which they would be exploring. Might the existence of a shared concern serve, in itself, to start a bonding process within any group?

Witnesses

To provide each group with information about the subject they were considering, each main jury day contained input from a number of witnesses who each gave a short presentation of their relevant knowledge and experience and were then available to the jury for questioning.

These witnesses were invariably senior people in their field who under normal circumstances would not expect to be cross-examined by ordinary members of the public! It probably says a lot about me and my 'authority figure' issues, but I have to admit I quite enjoyed seeing some of these witnesses struggle under the jury's blunt non-acceptance that something is the way it is because that's the way it is and therefore cannot change. Real public accountability in action.

The experience of the power that is engendered when a group works together brings up for me, in contrast, my sense of impotence as an individual to have any real impact on my own living or working conditions or environment.

Taking their power

A striking feature of all three groups for me has been the experience of witnessing a transformation in nervous, hesitant people (not least myself!). While all juries contained a number of people who were overtly confident and articulate, they also contained several who had valuable things to say and seemed at ease on a one-to-one basis but who tended, particularly in the early part of the process, to remain quiet during plenary sessions.

For one jury, frequent splitting into small groups seemed to provide a safe space for quieter jurors to express themselves less fearfully, gathering confidence as they went, eventually to participate more actively in the full group. I recall one young woman whose initial anxiety when speaking in the full jury was tangible. To say that she blossomed is no exaggeration and indeed she presented one section of the jury's final recommendations at a formal ceremony with the Leader of the Council. I believe that the experience of having her own and her peers' opinions and attitudes listened to and affirmed, gave her the confidence to express her views publicly with less anxiety.

Another jury, by the third day of four, voiced their own awareness of 'yappers' and quieter people and agreed, for the next session, that the 'yappers' should take a listening role.

All groups exercised the control we encouraged them to take over proceedings. Sessions were extended, extra witnesses were called, witnesses were recalled and small groupwork was convened only when the group decided to do so rather than happening automatically each day.

Having taken their power, the three juries produced practical and responsible recommendations which have been and still are being put into action.

Negativity

I think it would be fair to say that part of our jurors' motivation to agree to serve on a Citizens' Jury in the first place was that each was concerned about and had personal experience of the topic under discussion.

Inevitably, some of this experience and these opinions, were negative. It became evident to us very early in the process of the first jury that adequate space and attention had to be given to hearing and honouring this negative feeling with the same care more easily given to positivity. It felt clear that unless individuals received the opportunity to articulate the awfulness of their own stories, there was less space or willingness in them to consider other, different experiences or for them to step back from the detail of their particular circumstances to gain a more general picture.

While for Hugh, Kate and myself, the hearing of such negativity was important and necessary, it may not have felt helpful to some of the witnesses or to the council officials who were present as observers.

On a couple of occasions, this threw me into some confusion as I felt that my loyalties were being tested. While certain that my primary concern was firmly placed with the needs of the group, I also felt a loyalty to our client, the local authority, who were paying us. We wanted the project to go well and for them to commission us again – but several times they were smarting at some of the negativity expressed towards them, which we, they might argue, were encouraging and treating seriously.

At these times, I had to resist the temptation to 'make it better' for the Council (and ourselves?) and rely on my trust of the process that would ultimately produce the best for the client, though painful for them in that moment. I'm reminded of the analogy of the grazed knee – if the little bits of grit are not cleaned out of the wound, painful as that might be, the skin will not heal well.

Doubts

Across all three projects we have heard real surprise, incredulity and even scepticism that Citizens' Juries were 'for real'.

Jurors spoke openly of previous promises to 'listen to the people' – usually by prospective candidates at local and national elections: they promised you the earth when they wanted your vote – once they got it 'you never heard another word about it'.

One man, at an early coffee break, wanted to be certain that I knew he had never attended 'a big meeting' before. Was that really OK? In him, I sensed disbelief that participation from someone as 'unqualified' as he considered himself, could ever be taken seriously.

Another juror was certain one morning that his papers had been disturbed from the night before – one of 'them' must have been looking at his stuff. This had the potential for causing considerable difficulties, but could not be ignored.

All these doubts and suspicions had to be listened to if the overall assertion of the entire project was to be believed – that each jury member and his or her views and feelings mattered.

Staying with it

There was a significant moment in each of the juries (different in timing for each) when I sensed an urgency to move towards completion of the task. This seemed to emanate from recognition amongst jurors of the approaching boundary of time coupled with bewilderment and anxiety about how the group could possibly achieve an outcome.

This point of wanting to begin the ending, as it were, seemed to be preceded in each group by a sense of overwhelming chaos. In one jury, two very distinct and seemingly impenetrable 'camps' of opinion had developed, the force of the disagreement between them seeming to dominate proceedings. In another, a sense of the enormity of the problem seemed to depress all hope of the jury's ability to influence the situation. The words 'trust the process' seemed like a lifeline to me at these times.

Thousands of words had been heard and spoken, hundreds had been privately noted and publicly flip-charted. Discussions had been intense and focused as well as 'off on tangents' and maybe even irrelevant.

What now, with time running out?

Each jury came up with its own answer. For one, this meant splitting into the safety of their small groups to separately formulate recommendations which the whole group then drew together into consensus. The second jury chose to work as a whole group, first deciding on topic headings then working on the detail. Our 'hung' jury recognised and accepted themselves as divided and decided to separate into their two distinct groups to work on producing alternative sets of recommendations.

I now appreciate the huge importance of each group finding – and being facilitated to find – its own way to conclusion.

I will own that I took assumptions into the second group about how they would proceed, based on the experience of the first group. I had allowed myself to forget that a group is made up of individuals, no two of whom are alike, so how could I have assumed that two different groups would behave similarly? The answer is that I was temporarily seduced into designing methodology rather than being with people where they were and staying with them as they worked out how and where they wanted to go.

What can be relied upon, I believe from our three experiences, is that our faith that the group can achieve what it sets out to do, is in itself facilitative. This faith can stay with the chaos, seeing it as the place the process has led to and from where it will again move on.

Presentations

On the final day, jurors left us their written recommendations on flip-chart sheets. These we word-processed verbatim, together with a brief introduction by us and copies were circulated to all jurors, to give an opportunity to consider amendments. The final version was agreed at one final evening meeting. The Council funded a full colour print job on the document, the quality of which reflected the importance and seriousness of its content.

It has given me enormous satisfaction to attend the ceremonies at which the juries made formal presentations of their findings to the leaders of the local authorities. Each jury chose four or five members to present a flavour of different sections of their report before the formal handing over of their document. Yes, there was a lot a nervousness around but also a lot of energy and a desire to make their voices heard.

I clearly recall the first presentation and my feelings as the ceremony was just about to start. I was seated in the audience and my nervousness was reminiscent of a time many years ago as the curtain was about to rise on a school performance of *Joseph and His Technicolour Dreamcoat* in which my oldest daughter was performing. Wanting her to do as well as I knew she could – now I wanted these men and women to do themselves justice because I knew how hard they had worked and how well they had performed their task.

I recall the enthusiasm of my applause at the end of the presentation. I was so delighted by the clarity and obvious commitment of the jury spokespersons and the sincere appreciation with which their report was received by the Leader of the Council. To have been a part of what I had just witnessed in completion, was truly joyful.

Hope for the future

This commitment was really heard by the Council who have encouraged continued involvement by the jurors who wish to maintain their interest in the issue. Every juror also receives three-monthly progress updates on the implementation of their recommendations. The Council's genuine acknowledgement of the value of taking their leads directly from their electorate fills me with hope.

Public consultation via Citizens' Juries is not cheap, but if it produces decisions that emanate from the people whose lives those decisions affect, then who can argue the value of that?

The team

It has been a rich experience to be involved in this new way with two people whose work I greatly respect and with whom I already had other relationships. Kate and I became close friends while flatmates during our full-time Diploma in Counselling training which then led us into private practice together. In Kate's long and varied groupwork experience, I find confirmation of the person-centred approach, while Hugh's psychology background and market research expertise is a comforting and solid foundation on which the projects have been built.

Discussing team process recently with the others as I prepared to write about it here, I got in touch with a sense of disappointment that we didn't pay more attention at the time to what was developing between us. At the end of each jury, which took me away from normal life and work, it was easy to see 'catching up again' as my priority, rather than seeking time with Kate and Hugh to share our experiences of ourselves and each other. We have now given ourselves that opportunity, for which I'm grateful.

Some of the team dynamics bear mention. Because Hugh and I are married, it is inevitable that we talk about work at times when Kate is not present. This has potential for difficulty, as we sometimes appeared to exclude her. It felt good that she was able to say this.

Another pairing exists between Kate and me through our shared person-centred approach and the experience of training and working together. This shows up in our ability to communicate almost in a kind of shorthand to which Hugh is not privy, resulting in his asking for explanation and clarification. On one occasion during the second jury, late in the evening as we processed the day, I am aware that I reacted quite aggressively. I believe this comes from a frustration in me that I sometimes find it difficult to articulate my 'way of being' in words that make sense to someone who is coming from a different place. I want Hugh to understand but my explanations can fall short of making sense to him. It feels like I don't need to explain to Kate – she's coming from the same place. Would I react differently to Hugh's challenge if we were not married? I can only guess 'yes', but our relationship is close in so many other ways and we want to be able to work with our differences.

We have also been able to explore issues within the team, not exactly of power, but something of that ilk. The invitation to become involved in this work came to Hugh as a result of his considerable background of research work for Scottish local authorities. It was his project, as it were. I heard about it thanks to a casual suppertime remark and asked to see the written brief. Well, then I was up and running! What I read was about the empowerment of the ordinary person, decision making by the people for the people – music to my political and person-centred ears – and, after making a significant contribution to our successful written proposal for the project, I felt a degree of ownership too. For Kate, involvement came at a stage when much had already been discussed between Hugh and me and also with the local authority.

I am also now very aware that the market research element of the project – the recruitment process and the administrative component – was an unknown for Kate. We were all equally unfamiliar with the actual jury format but Kate was also new to the bits that felt very safe for Hugh and me. I didn't appreciate at the time how this would affect Kate who at times felt useless and 'not part of' as Hugh and I scurried around being busy, knowing what we were doing.

In our team preparation before the first jury actually sat, we didn't address this power dimension – unaware, I suppose, of its pertinence or impact for each of us. It is now part of our team strength that we have addressed the feelings this engendered. Such expression and three shared experiences have moved us on into what feels to me like much more equal positions.

And finally . . .

I would like to end with the words of a juror as we were saying goodbye. He was a manager of a local leisure facility with a team of staff. Expressing his pleasure at having been part of a Citizens' Jury, he chose to comment specifically on the movement, as he had experienced it, of a group of strangers with widely disparate points of view, over the course of four and a half days together, from difference to consensus. He wished he could get to that point with his staff. Summing up our involvement, he concluded: 'You must have done something – but I don't know what!'

Reference:

Coote, A. and Lenaghan, J. (1997). *Citizens' Juries: Theory into practice*. London: Institute for Public Policy Research.

LARGE GROUPS AND WORKSHOPS

The FDI (Britain) Workshops

8

John Barkham

Background and history

The FDI Summer Workshops took place in Britain between 1975 and 1995. Residential, lasting from seven to ten days, they offered 'experience and theory in facilitating groups'. The brochure described the first one's purpose, 'to provide an intensive learning experience in which the participants can discover their own power and resources, find strength and support for their personal and professional lives, and explore new ways of working with individuals and groups'. A later brochure suggests, 'We anticipate that the workshop will have a primary training function for those who work with individuals or groups, yet will also provide a context for personal growth and development.' As such, the workshops can be viewed as temporary educational institutions whose purpose was to promote and develop individuals' capacity to meet fully the challenges of their outside personal and professional lives – hence *Facilitator Development Institute* (FDI).

The first staff group of the FDI (Britain) Summer Workshop comprised Charles (Chuck) Devonshire, William Hallidie Smith, Elke Lambers, Dave Mearns and Brian Thorne. The latter three members were counsellors and groupwork practitioners in Britain, while Chuck Devonshire was a member of the Centre for Studies of the Person, founded by Carl Rogers in La Jolla, California. Consistent with their person-centred approach, the staff's consultant was Carl Rogers. They also appointed a researcher, John McLeod, to emphasise their interest in and commitment to learning about the results of the workshop process and individual learning outcomes. This work was subsequently produced in the form of a PhD thesis (McLeod, 1977).

Prior to the 1983 workshop, the staff announced their intention to discontinue their role, together with their wish to explore with previous participants the future of the workshops. As a result, a new staff group of five emerged through that week and a follow-up weekend. Their role was to continue to organise, manage and staff future workshops. The five individuals were variously working in counselling and education in England, Northern Ireland and Scotland. They were

John Barkham, Jenny Bell, Prue Conradi, Mhairi MacMillan and Willie Thompson. All had attended previous workshops and, in two cases, had been in the role of trainee staff. They proceeded to offer workshops in July of each year 1984–95. Later, they developed the Winter Holiday Workshop. This was offered around Christmas time each year, 1988–96, in Morocco or the Canary Islands.

The workshops offered the possibility of experience in small groups and large community meetings without a specific agenda. In addition, more focused subjects for exploration centred on the interests of individual staff members. Numbers attending the workshops during the 70s and early 80s varied between 50 and 100, providing a minimum number that was consistent with most people's idea of a 'large group'. In the late 80s and early 90s, it proved more difficult to recruit. Group size varied from 16 to 38. Another changing feature of the membership was the workshop becoming decreasingly international. In the early years, 15 countries were represented. The increasing development of broadly similar workshops on the European continent probably accounts for this trend. In the later years, almost all participants were from the United Kingdom. A very large majority of participants were highly educated, middle class, middle-aged and white. A limited number of bursaries were offered to enable students and those on low incomes to attend.

The reduction in the number attending, despite a considerable marketing effort, may indicate a declining interest in this form of unstructured groupwork since the death of Carl Rogers. It is important to note that most participants were self-funded, taking holiday time, and generally had to weigh up carefully their personal priorities of time and expenditure. It is also possible that during the more hard-headed 90s a clientele, once giving priority to personal development work, now seeks financial support from training budgets.These enable the pursuit of more overtly professional goals through workshops advertising more clearly-defined and more readily explicable outcomes. In addition, most of the diverse, broadly humanistic workshops now on offer focus on specific areas of personal exploration or human endeavour.

I attended the workshops in the summers of 1981 and 1983 and, as a staff member, 1984–95, together with the winter ones 1988–91. At every workshop at least two staff members were present as facilitators. On only one occasion (summer 1988) were all five staff present. Inevitably, my reflections are personal ones rather than representing the views and experience of my colleagues.

Structure
The Summer Workshops
The workshops may have been unique in their combination of annual, residential context and participant-defined structure. The latter needs clarification. In the brochure for the last summer workshop, the following statement is made: 'Only the initial stages of the workshop will be structured by the staff. House meal-times provide further structural framework. Otherwise, the programme is created by the group working together in such a way that the needs of each individual can be taken into account.' The staff determined the time of arrival and registration,

and of the first meeting of the whole group or community. Normally they were the first to speak at this meeting, introducing themselves with thoughts and feelings about the workshop and their hopes for it. Any essential housekeeping points were also made. Members often followed with similar personal introductory statements. Less often, the urgent personal or emotional business of one or more members rapidly intervened. It would be true to say that throughout these groups primacy was given to feelings rather than to intellectual expression. This was in spite of frequent statements against the development of a tyranny in which only feelings were acceptable currency.

Introductions are a very obvious and explicit form of *arrival* process. Anxiety levels are often high at the start of workshops. When there is less obvious and imposed structure, participants frequently experience this acutely. In FDI workshops there was often a rush, particularly from new participants, towards 'getting a programme organised', with divisions into small groups and timetables. Small groups are often seen as a haven of escape from the anxiety of participating in the large group where all participants and staff are present. Such pressures exerted by the anxiety of uncertainty were often resisted by more experienced participants, resulting in early interpersonal conflicts, hurt, and the need to attend to the range of feelings that resulted.

In the summer workshops the large group or 'community' generally met throughout the morning, for part of the afternoon and after supper in the evenings of the first two days. The desire for small, ongoing groups, each with a facilitator became increasingly urgent business through this early period. The timing of a decision to achieve this splitting varied enormously from one workshop to another, as did the actual mechanism for forming small groups.The dilemmas of choosing and, in so doing, rejecting other opportunities (and people) were felt painfully by many. In only one workshop did the whole group choose to stay together throughout the week.

When a programme was finally agreed within the whole group, each succeeding day generally held to a similar pattern. Typically, the whole group met together first thing in the morning and after supper in the evening. Ongoing small groups followed coffee, there was free time after lunch, and then a variety of small groups and workshops took place in the period between tea and supper. It is difficult to evaluate the extent to which the similarity of such an emerging programme between years reflected genuinely similar wishes among different groups of participants. It is also possible that staff, colluding subconsciously with previous participants, exerted pressure to reach a balance that satisfied their needs and objectives. In my own case, this commonly occurring balance of activities met my needs.

Here is an illustration of a conscious staff attempt to develop a different structure. By 1992, we shared a feeling of some weariness with the necessarily slow beginning-process of the workshops and the fact that a sensible programme generally took so long to emerge. For the 1993 workshop we therefore proposed a new design. We proposed a central focus and theme of *learning and facilitation in groupwork – experience and reflection*. We proposed that the workshop would consist of a mixture of large and small group meetings, with specific periods set aside for reflective discussion particularly focusing on aspects of facilitative behaviour. Small groups were to be of equal size, each with a member of staff, with individuals allocated to them by staff in advance of the workshop. Each small-group member would also act as facilitator for one of the group's sessions and all sessions would end with a period for reflection. Thus the workshop was designed with a particular training function in mind. It proved to be one of the most difficult workshops we ran. The possible reasons for this are evaluated later.

The Winter Holiday Workshops

An earlier attempt to change the traditional minimalist staff determination of structure was developed in the winter holiday workshops. A pattern of whole group and small group meetings for every day throughout the week was suggested in advance. Afternoon and evening free time was scheduled in order to take full advantage of the holiday element of what was advertised. Somewhat to our surprise, participants never contested this 'offer' of greater structure, welcoming not having to negotiate the groups and the timetable. It released participants to explore their personal and interpersonal issues in other ways. However, there remained for the assembled membership the task of splitting into the small groups. The structure of the winter workshop remained almost unchanged throughout the years it ran.

It is likely that a lack of structure plunges participants more rapidly into deep areas of anxiety about issues of power, authority, leadership and boundaries. If these are carefully and thoroughly explored, they give rise to extremely important learning for living in the outside world. Conversely, an imposed structure gives rise to a greater degree of safety and the possibility of a range of different issues being explored.

The role of staff

At an early point in the workshops, the role of staff was often questioned. Staff who do not provide an agenda or a timetable, nor 'maintain order' can be seen – especially by new members, and despite the carefully written brochure – as professionally inept. At a deeper level such feelings may be interpreted as childlike in the face of 'parents' failing to take control. Most hierarchical organisations seek to maintain those of lower status in a perpetual state of powerless immaturity and most in such positions expect to be there. FDI workshops provided a revolutionary challenge to this model, inviting participants to share with staff the task of determining the process and content of the workshop. It was a reasonable question for participants to ask, therefore, 'What are the staff doing?'

The role of the person-centred facilitator of a large group is complex and challenging. It has been described in numerous works by Rogers (e.g., 1973, 1978). A major issue that has been little addressed is the extent to which it can be trained for. All of the five staff had undertaken counselling and groupwork training. Together we had also gained a very considerable amount of experience as participants, not only in person-centred groups. Yet I remember vividly the level of stress I experienced in the first workshop we staffed together. I had a splitting headache almost throughout. I also remember moments and behaviours of mine in the early years of being a staff member that caused me acute embarrassment. They can only be excused in the context of being human, taking risks, making mistakes, and learning from experience. I know that no amount of training could have prevented this process. Rather, it indicated to me my own lack of maturity and the need to address fully a whole raft of personal issues with which I had not yet fully dealt. The belief that a 'how to do it' training provides the wherewithal necessary and sufficient for the work is an easy trap in which to fall.

I have experienced occasionally in other workshops facilitators using technique only to mask the congruence and vulnerability essential for staff to be experienced as trustworthy and competent. There is no substitute for personal work. It is a fundamental part of the training of an adequate person-centred facilitator. The depth and demands placed upon staff in a week-long event are such that personal shortcomings are quickly exposed. This is an inevitable result of the crucible, the severe trial for staff that a workshop becomes. If this were not so, the depths reached, the work done, and the results achieved by and for individuals will be of limited value.

These comments can be viewed within the overall context of the great challenge facing all person-centred practitioners of managing the personal-professional boundary. The professional task cannot be satisfactorily addressed without full and open access to the whole person; it can be readily abused without a sensitive containment of personal issues.

The staff developed the discipline of meeting on the Thursday evening before the Saturday afternoon start of the summer workshops. This gave us time to make the transition from our outside lives and tune in to one another. It also enabled us to determine specific roles like who was to start the first community meeting and which of us were prepared to facilitate small groups and special topic workshops. There were also housekeeping and administrative tasks to attend to. We experienced the tuning-in process being of vital importance to ensure that we were aware of each other's current issues, could give support to each other when necessary, and could address any interpersonal issues.

There were two occasions when we failed to complete this business adequately before the beginning of the workshop. The first was the 1990 winter workshop. It was not usually possible for the staff to meet more than 24 hours before the winter workshops. On this occasion, two of the staff arrived in a state of virtual exhaustion. They were hardly in a fit state to withstand the unusual level of aggression directed towards them on that particular occasion by a small group of members. A charge of incompetence was levelled as a result.

The second occasion was the 1993 summer workshop with its specific new structure and purpose. It transpired that the staff group did not have the level of collective agreement about, and commitment to, the process we thought we had fully negotiated. Further, there were personal conflicts between us that were not resolved within the staff group and were not openly aired within the community.

This created substantial confusion, again leading to attempts to divide the staff and to charges of incompetence. Two staff members dealing with extremely stressful circumstances from their personal lives served to add to a sense that the staff collectively were unable to 'hold' the energies of the community (see the evaluations below).

These isolated experiences serve to demonstrate the effects of the particular disposition of staff individually and collectively on the workshop process as a whole. After the difficult winter workshop of 1990, one member wrote afterwards about his experience:

> 'One view about what went wrong is that two staff members were too exhausted, distressed and preoccupied by difficulties in their own lives to facilitate as they would have wished. Because the staff did not make it clear what they would and would not do as facilitators, they created a dependent group unable to free any member who offered to take an initiative for the group. Instead they actively blocked others from usurping the power they refused to own or share. Their personal paralysis was projected into the group, so that they dis-facilitated any potential for healing, mutual support or development among others. Thus the group was disempowered from the start.'

Whether or not one agrees with the specifics of this analysis, it demonstrates correctly that mismanaged personal-professional boundaries by staff lead to great distress and confusion. However, a negative response to the effectiveness of staff or to the workshop as a whole needs to be separated from learning outcomes. These could be powerful and positive in the area of managing power and authority in the light of difficult and painful experience.

Following this particular workshop, in order to respond to a participant's challenge in a letter to me, I wrote down what I could about the role of staff as I experienced it:

> Staff alone cannot create a climate of trust but, by the example of their behaviour, they can at best show everyone the way. The sort of behaviour that begins to engender that trust and which I try to adopt involves me:
>
> • listening attentively and making this apparent through the response I make, which may be a verbal one, but might also be through eye contact, a nod or a smile;
>
> • treating with respect the contribution that any person may make to the activity of the group. This means acknowledging it, checking it out if I do not understand it; accepting it as valid and meant by that person, even if I do not share that particular point of view; challenging it if I feel damaged or hurt by it or if I see another person suffering as a result of it. A contribution may be a silent one, and it may be an action rather than words. Each of us has our own way of contributing,

and this is deserving of respect;

• acting in a way that is genuine. This means being in touch with my feelings, noting them as I go along, registering what they mean – as far as I can understand them – in relation to what is going on for me in the group. I may or may not choose to express or act on my feelings, according to whether on balance I feel it is likely to be helpful to others. If I do decide to respond actively to my feelings or thoughts, I try to do so in a way that is consistent with them and which, therefore, shows to others how I feel. If I behave in a way that is inconsistent with how I feel, I am experienced as confusing or false;

• helping others as best I can to make sense of their and other people's experience. One of the hardest things to achieve through careful, active listening is an understanding of how it feels to be that other person. This means trying to set aside my experience, my tendency to pigeon-hole someone or the way they are into my well-established intellectual framework and assumptions, and really trying to feel what they feel like. If I can express this, or struggle towards it with their help, it may help them too – 'Aha, yes, that's it; that's it exactly!';

• staying in the present, the 'here and now'. I may wish to refer to past, future and outside events but, by and large, I shall want to attend to my own and others' thoughts and feelings as they occur. It is easy to escape from the difficulty, pain or embarrassment as well as from the joy and excitement of the present by lapsing into the anecdotal. I shall try not to be this way. I want to be here, now, with my fullest energies.

It may be very difficult for some people to cope with a staff member being like this. This is especially so for those used to being led, who want to be looked after, protected from their own difficult feelings or those of others, or who feel they have paid a lot of money and expect the staff 'to do something' – like setting up small groups, putting people into them, arranging all the times when they are to meet, and giving them an agenda to discuss.

Such a statement is readily recognisable as not too dissimilar from one a person-centred therapist might make. It describes a way in which others may be empowered, encouraged to value their own and others' experience, and enter equally into a negotiating process that will, at best, result in a great variety of individual needs being met. The goal, or maybe 'an impossible challenge' for the staff member, is to achieve this with all members of a group, not just one person. A condition of participation written in the brochure was that a workshop 'is not a substitute for psychotherapy or counselling. Participants are in all ways taking part because of their own free will, and are fully responsible for themselves during the workshop.' There may be personal therapeutic outcomes – perhaps inevitably so, not least among staff if they are properly open to their experience – but a staff member is not therapist and does not carry the responsibility that accompanies that role.

The exercise of power

Issues of power dynamics in person-centred groups merit much deeper and more extensive evaluation than is possible in this chapter. Here, I give just a very few other insights arising from my experience.

Abuses of power in all kinds of organisation – commerce, industry, church, health, education – are as readily recognisable at all levels as they are ubiquitous. This does not excuse them, but it may be easier to avoid or contest what is obvious. There are real dangers in the leadership of person-centred groups of hidden abuses of power. This is because a fundamental tenet is to share power. Through stating and believing this as a staff member, it is easy to enter denial about the power one is exerting and which is experienced by participants. I am sure I was guilty of this on more than one occasion in relation to isolated incidents. However, my sense is that this was not a frequent or consistent experience in FDI workshops. If it had been, the workshops would have proved damaging experiences for participants. There is some evidence that this was manifestly not the case in terms of the considerable number of participants who attended more than one event. Nevertheless, if staff achieve the letting go and sharing of the reins of power in the group that they purport to do, one has to accept the possibility of persons experiencing acute anxiety and periods of chaos, frustration and confusion. Staff may experience the danger of the event being perceived as a failure and the staff incompetent.

However, whereas instances of abuses of power may, at least in retrospect, be readily identifiable, the extent to which staff behaviour is empowering is more difficult to assess. This is complicated by the fact that staff are experienced as powerful, often much more so than they themselves suspect. There are real dangers of staff becoming gurus, so determined sometimes are the undercurrents of powerlessness and the desire to project personal authority on to a leader figure and develop a dependency culture. Whereas I feel confident that neither I nor any of my colleagues encouraged *gurudom*, all of us were looked to in more subtle ways for leadership, guidance, support, and for providing some sort of safe limits to the activities and behaviours that took place (see the evaluations below).

It was my experience as a participant that there were more extreme and bizarre behaviours during the workshops run by the first staff group in the 70s than in those run by me and my four colleagues in the 80s. This is not a criticism of either. Rather, it raises a variety of possible reasons – the cultural differences between the 70s and the 80s; the size of groups, which were much larger in the 70s; the more international flavour of the earlier groups; and the unconscious limits to behaviour imposed by the staff. These may be limits set by an unacknowledged recognition of staff capacity or unwillingness to cope with such behaviour. This is a possible example of the hidden power of staff.

More obvious exercise of power emanates from the range of staff behaviours described above which, when consistently experienced, add up to a powerful image and presence. This in itself can be disempowering – 'leave it to the facilitators – they will know how to deal with it.' Workshop staff, by being effective, can inadvertently cumulatively acquire a power that diminishes what should be an empowering experience for participants.This may be a strong argument for no staff team holding the reins for too long. It is at least arguable that the team of which I was a member, and which organised 20 workshops, did just this.

We worked well together, in different combinations, enjoyed being together doing the work, and only came together *for* this work from our domains scattered across the kingdom. We were resistant to involving others in the staff role, either to take our places or to act as trainees. Whilst we did this on two occasions, it was only because of clashes with our other personal and professional commitments.

Outcomes for participants

Carl Rogers' books published in the 70s and early 80s encouraged the belief that the person-centred approach was bringing about a revolution in human behaviour in a very wide range of individual and organisational endeavour. In his last years, Rogers was deeply involved in groupwork with a distinctly political agenda – in Northern Ireland, Russia and South Africa. He seemed optimistic that his way of being and working could and would make a difference. It is difficult to evaluate his degree of success in such a grandiose project. It is arguable that his impact at this level was negligible and that the human world is at least as nasty as it ever was.

On the other hand, there is plenty of evidence from workshop evaluations to suggest that the impact of effectively-managed person-centred groupwork has profoundly influenced the life of many individuals in directions that they consider strongly positive. There are also those who have been left feeling alienated, even damaged by the experience. At best, one must assume that the positive impacts on individuals will reverberate through the activities of their lives, making their contributions to society positive ones. It is hopeful to believe that, thereby, the contribution made by the workshops forms part of the solution to human social dilemmas rather than part of the problem. I think this is a realistic assessment.

We made a systematic attempt to evaluate the experience of participants in just two workshops – the first winter workshop (1988) and the difficult summer one (1993). In each case this was immediately at the end of the event. The results of the 1988 evaluation suggest almost entirely positive outcomes at the endpoint of the workshop. They might be regarded as typical of an event whose overall chemistry worked well. The statements in Box 1 are broadly typical.

After the 1990 winter workshop, a participant wrote some two months later, 'It was not a happy experience for me but it was one of great learning.' It is worth emphasising that much valuable learning may only result from a necessarily painful passage. This is important for an educational institution, however much happy outcomes for members may be desired.

The evaluation of the 1993 workshop was an extensive one and amounted to about 10,000 words from 22 of the 27 members. These were in response to the following questions:

> Comment on your hopes and expectations before the workshop and the extent to which these have been fulfilled:
>
> • In what ways has the workshop been of benefit to you – useful things you have learned?
>
> • In what ways do you imagine you might want to change your work and personal relationships as a result of what you have learned?
>
> • What key incidents during the workshop stand out for you?
>
> • Who were the key people for you at the workshop, and why were they so important?
>
> • What have you learned about facilitative behaviour – in general, yours and others?
>
> • What has communication with back-home people been like, during and since the workshop?
>
> • How do you feel now?
>
> • Your overall evaluation of the workshop.

Inevitably I give only the briefest selection of comments (found in Box 2), principally in response to the first and last questions. They illustrate many of the points of a more general kind that I have already made.

Box 1: Evaluative comments from participants of the 1988 FDI Winter Holiday Workshop

- I'm unambiguously glad I joined the workshop. I feel unfolded.
- It was a valuable experience, in terms of self-awareness and in the way groups and individuals transact.
- I enjoyed myself. Many thanks for your brilliantly subtle contribution to a successful week.
- Enjoyed it enormously – restorative community atmosphere and opportunity which I took for individual release.
- An extremely valuable experience – it's difficult to explain why, but it was important to be away from England. There was a timelessness which helped me to live in the present and be myself. I can honestly say it was the happiest and most helpful week of my life.
- Entirely good. A wonderful sharing experience. Just about the right combination of sybaritic holiday and hard personal work.
- Splendidly organised and facilitated.
- This has been a valuable experience for me which I am still processing. I'm really glad I came.

Box 2: Evaluative comments from participants of the 1993 FDI Summer Workshop

- My main hope was to be clearer about the ways that groups function and how they can be facilitated. These hopes were fulfilled to some extent.
- It was like seeing all my previous training experience come alive in front of me, and make sense.
- I felt, through the workshop, the beginnings of an understanding of person-centred. How important it is to acknowledge the differences between us – this, most forcibly, has stayed with me and hopefully will be of benefit.
- I have learned still more about the value of staying with the group process and how very difficult that can be. I thought about conflict and felt it possibly arose because of different expectations by both staff and participants, of learning through experience and/or through training. It would seem in this situation that staff need to be particularly clear about their aims and process.
- A learning process spoiled by the loss of intellectual content. Your advertised intention to offer a structure with a more explicit training function was lost in the new/old and head/heart conflicts.
- I am very grateful I could attend. Some people said they did not feel safe and I wonder whether it was because, not only were they sometimes not well heard, but also that they sensed as I did that the facilitators were often not at peace with themselves and sometimes not with each other.
- I found the workshop excellent. I felt an atmosphere of dissatisfaction (although I don't know why). I also felt there was disharmony and dissatisfaction coming from the facilitators. Again, I don't know why. I did not feel any of these things myself. My small group only seemed to work for a few people but this was because others did not wish to participate. Perhaps the large group never formed and didn't become completely safe. Neither of these affected me.
- I was glad and relieved that at NO time at all was there any pressure on me to share parts of myself I didn't wish to share. In small groups I *think* I would have liked a more in-depth, analytical exploration of all those mysterious processes that were going on.
- From all the expectations I had, the one which stands out most is the time and the space available to me to get in touch with my feelings. At the same time, the expectation that group (small and big) members allow me to be myself by listening, acknowledging and understanding. By the end of the week I remember feeling that these expectations were met.
- I have had a number of aspects of my 'true' self reflected back by a new

set of individuals and that was re-affirming. I can begin to believe in myself again.

- I used the opportunity in making relationships with men and women to explore important issues for me – power boundaries, sexuality and intimate connections.
- 'Modelling' of the core conditions was of benefit to me. I have learned – to stay with the difficulties, to use my inner strength/resources. It has helped me process some of the confusion I had from participating in a previous groupwork course.
- The turning point in my life.

Overall, perhaps these comments point more than anything else towards the extraordinary variety of personal agendas with which participants come, together with the uniquely variable and personal responses to the experience. It is a radically different one for each person present.

However, collectively they also indicate that the staff inadvertently set up a 'split' model that resulted in a conflict played out by the participants in this workshop. This conflict was between those who had been previous participants and were anxious about losing the rich unstructured experience, and those who were new and came for a 'training event'.

Recent developments

The FDI Workshops ended with the summer one of 1995. Billed as the last one, it was well attended. However, no firm proposals were made for some alternative continuation. This may have been partly because of the ambiguous message presented by the 'retiring' staff in that they expressed the intention of holding on to the name 'FDI'.

Subsequently, however, a small group of experienced past participants spent a weekend together to discuss ways in which to develop the concept and put a new initiative into practice. As a result, a week-long workshop for the summer of 1997 was arranged in which it was agreed that participants would be personally invited by those present at the planning meeting. There would be no designated facilitators. It was made clear to all participants that the responsibility for care and attention to others was a shared one. Twenty-two people attended. At a subsequent planning meeting it was agreed that membership of future workshops would be achieved through networking, each member of the previous one being entitled to invite one other. At the time of writing, the maximum of 29 allowed by the accommodation has been achieved for the July 1998 workshop, together with a substantial waiting-list.

This new development seems to reflect a maturing of the concept of the FDI workshops. No longer is it necessary to have designated staff members. The withdrawal of the 'parents' allows others to show their effectiveness. This requires a fully adult acceptance of responsibility shared among the membership. The challenges of a lack of prearranged structure and timetable still remain.

Acknowledgements

I am very grateful to my FDI staff colleagues for their forbearance over many years; to Mhairi MacMillan for her editorial guidance; and to Gillian Feest and Adrian Foote for their stimulating thoughts and discussion.

References

McLeod, J. (1977). Unpublished PhD Thesis, University of Edinburgh.
Rogers, C. (1973). *Carl Rogers on Encounter Groups*. Harmondsworth: Penguin.
Rogers, C. (1978). *Carl Rogers on Personal Power*. London: Constable.

Toward an Understanding of Large Group Dialogue and its Implications

9

John Keith Wood

The act of knowing
is an evolutionary development
of the phenomenon and
not just a subjective activity of the mind

Henri Bortoft
on the thought of
J.W. von Goethe

Large groups have obvious survival advantages over smaller ones. Improved opportunities for nutrition and security are enough to suggest that large groups would seem to have been favored by human evolution. In this regard, the British psychologist Robin Dunbar (1996), who has made significant contributions to biological anthropology, has proposed that *human language* itself evolved due to the necessity of maintaining large groups. Doubtless, large groups have played an intimate role in the evolution of the species, and continue to do so.

This chapter deals with temporary large groups that convene participants for up to 12 hours per day for a week or two with the intention of exploring a topic of interest – which most often is themselves and their relationships. To understand such an event – and more generally, the phenomenon of large groups – one must consider, among other things: the membership of the group; participants' relationships with each other, and to the group itself; where, under what conditions, for what duration, and for what purpose the group has been constituted. Also, it would help to know if one is speaking about a 'successful' or 'unsuccessful' group activity and by what criteria this characterization has been established.[1]

In considering this vast subject, it may be useful to begin by establishing a notion of largeness. In dealing with this aspect, guidelines for effectiveness also emerge.

How big is large?

The specific size of any group may not be as relevant as the relationship that members have with one another and the circumstances that surround their gathering. For example, one could imagine becoming overwhelmed by a relatively small number of people, in a crowded urban labyrinth; or perhaps feeling comfortable with an enormous number, especially were the new 'Internet' promises to be fully realized.[2]

To address this question from the point of view of the individual, the reported counsel of Aristotle is relevant: *If a person cries for help at the center, and is not heard on the periphery, the group is too large.*

Plato is said to have answered the question of the maximum number of participants in a large group, that would be constructive for the collective, in this way: *I would allow the state to increase so far as is consistent with unity; that, I think, is the proper limit.*

I consider the intersection of these (often considered contradictory, but apparently complementary) descriptions to be all that is necessary to define, broadly, an effective large group workshop and its size.

Thus, a large group that may be effective within a series of criteria already suggested in an earlier article (Wood, 1997) would be:

1. One in which each of its members may be 'heard on the periphery'. That is, able to express himself or herself and has the possibility of being felt understood by the entire group. It is a context in which a participant's best ideas are seriously considered. This implies that one also has a responsibility (and equally important, cultivates an increasing ability) to listen to others in a like manner.

2. One in which individuals, while fully in touch with their personal identities, are also capable of operating, at the same time, in a state of consciousness in which *the unity of the group may be perceived as the most significant referent.*

Thus, participants would fight for their personal idea, for their private point of view, and then surrender it willingly for a better one that may help the group move towards its goals. Individual group members would accept their own contradictory values as well as those of others *and* integrate them for constructive purposes (Wood, 1984). If such a 'split-brain' proposal seems preposterous, one may consult the research that suggests that a normal person may relatively easily learn to read with adequate speed and comprehension on one subject while s*imultaneously* writing on *another* subject (Hirst, Neisser and Spelke, 1978).

The resultant unity in its complete sense is not merely imposed by the mind. As the studies of the German savant J.W. von Goethe have suggested, 'It is the wholeness of the phenomenon itself. The unity *is* the phenomenon' (Bortoft, 1996).

Numbers

The French sociologist Gustov LeBon (1895) has asserted that the crowd is not dependent on numbers but on the 'disappearance of conscious personality'. Doubtless there is a diminishment of 'conscious personality' in a state of consciousness that allows one to perceive the group's unity. Likewise, there is doubtless a diminishment of 'conscious sociability' in that state of consciousness which we know as isolation, a person alone with his or her thoughts. Whatever the perspective, the ideal number of participants in an effective group would answer the question, 'In this situation, how many participants who are able to actualize the best qualities of both their individual and social selves can be accommodated?'

In more recent history, 'being heard' has been emphasized when considering the optimum number of participants in a group. The American psychologist Jack Gibb (a pioneer in the development of personal and interpersonal learning for normal people in large groups) has related that in 'T-groups' in the 1940's and 50's, 10 or 12 participants would meet together and very soon someone would suggest, 'Let's break into smaller groups.' It was explained, 'I am freer to discuss and express myself with just two or three others' (see Bradford, Gibb and Benne, 1964).

In the late 1960's, I moved to La Jolla, California, and participated in the La Jolla Program, annual sessions held for some 100 participants to learn to be encounter group facilitators. There were one or two brief large-group meetings of all participants during two weeks in which the organizers had divided the population into small encounter groups of 10 or 12. They believed 'real encounter' took place in the small groups. The plenary sessions were thought of as a mere novelty (Rogers, 1970).

In 1977, at a workshop organized by the Brazilian psychologist Eduardo Bandeira that American psychologists Carl Rogers, Maria and Jack Bowen, Maureen O'Hara and I convened with some 800 participants in Rio de Janeiro, several participants expressed the desire to break into smaller groups where they imagined they would feel more intimate. Thus, the one large group was divided into five smaller groups of some 160 or so persons each. My own feeling, gazing at the people in my 'small' group, was definitely more relaxed and more trusting. The group began an encounter whose characteristics resembled those of groups of 10 or 12 in La Jolla.

Summarizing, a 'large' group was considered to number 10 or 12 to some people at a certain time and place. This figure was thought of as 'small' to other people in another time and place who felt 100 or so would constitute a large group. Later, this amount seemed small to another population in another time and place for whom 800 or so would be considered large.

Perhaps a working definition for size would be the following: a large group is one that involves a sufficient number of participants that each spends considerably more time listening than speaking. However, this number is not so great that the individual's voice cannot be 'heard on the periphery', nor does its size prevent the possibility of participants perceiving the 'unity'.

From various experiences in North and South America and Europe, I would put (for sake of discussion) the number of participants that would generally constitute a large group at around the size of a small-town community meeting or a local church congregation: between 50 and 300, an agreeable mean of, say, 150.[3]

The approach that oriented the large group workshops considered here
The large group workshops and their meetings that will be considered were organized from a perspective called, 'the person-centered approach'. Both for readers who have no idea what this means, as well as for those who assume they do know, I would like to briefly state its meaning for this chapter.

The fact that the phrase, 'the person-centered approach' came into common usage around 1974, when it would be applied to a hodgepodge of activities, has obscured both its historical and, more importantly, its practical significance.[4]

Currently, the essential approach is almost universally misunderstood. Replete with category errors in its usage, the term 'person-centered approach' may denote almost anything, from a 'science', to a 'philosophy', to a 'political movement', even to a body of followers of tenets that resemble a religion. It is pursued as a 'method of counseling', as a 'professional status', as membership in a 'school of thought', and as a personal 'identity'. Anything, it seems, except merely what it is, an *approach.*

Even worse, due to the chronological development of the name, analogies suggesting that the approach is the superficial and colorful foliage of a tree whose roots are the ample and reliable client-centered therapy are abundant.

Whereas, this image should be turned upside down.

The person-centered approach may be more precisely and more constructively conceived of as the 'root' of a 'tree' whose principal 'branch' is client-centered therapy.

Other branches are student-centered education; small group encounter for personal growth; large group workshops for transnational understanding, for the resolution of intergroup conflicts and, most important, for learning (largely through large-group workshops) about culture, its formation and transformation.

Carl Rogers's most important achievement, in spite of a long and distinguished career as a psychotherapist, may not have been so much the development of a successful method for effective psychotherapy in a particular time and place. It may have been the cultivation of this *approach* that could be applied creatively by people at various times and places, under various circumstances, in various endeavors.

The person-centered approach, briefly
This approach, this stance, this 'way of being', as Rogers (1980) eventually summarized the constellation of *beliefs, attitudes* and *values,* and *abilities* that were enhanced by experience, was rooted, 'not in truth already known or formulated but in the process by which truth is dimly perceived, tested and approximated' (Rogers, 1974).

Rogers (1980) *believed* in a 'formative directional tendency' in the universe. A person could be trusted to know what was best for his or her 'personal growth'.

And, given certain conditions, would move toward that goal.

He also *relied* on the implications of this belief for groups. Although, within the more volatile group activities, confidence in this hypothesis had to be regained in each experience.

Rogers's *attitude* included a tolerance for ambiguity. Keats's (1899, p. 277) Shakespeare is the model with his, *'negative capability . . .* capable of being in uncertainties, mysteries, doubts, without any irritable reaching after fact and reason'.

Also, Rogers respected the people he participated with in therapy or groups as equals in their essential humanity and attempted to meet them without pretense or design, merely as 'persons'.

He was curious about human nature and wanted to learn from encounters with others. He was also willing, within reason, *to be changed* by that experience: in the vein that the Austrian-Israeli philosopher Martin Buber (1966) had proposed, 'I felt I have not the right to want to change another, if I am not open to be changed by him as far as it is legitimate'.

Rogers's specific *abilities* were enhanced from confrontations of the aforementioned beliefs and attitudes with the phenomenon of psychotherapy; others from education; others, from small and large-group encounters.

In general, Rogers developed an ability to intensely concentrate and clearly grasp the linear, piece-by-piece, appearance of reality while at the same time possessing an *esprit de finesse*, not having to break things into parts, but being able to seize the experience so as to perceive its direct meaning and character.

In summary, each activity assumed a unique formulation of his 'way of being', which then became both a means and an end to its constructive outcome. Rogers's personal, interpersonal and transpersonal approach was the same: *He turned the best part of himself toward the best part of the other in order that something of lasting value might be accomplished that none could have done alone* (Wood, 1995).

Large group workshops
As already mentioned, since 1967 the La Jolla Program had been training encounter group leaders. To supplement the structured program of small group encounters, brief plenary sessions were held. These meetings demonstrated that it was possible for over 100 persons to speak in one significant conversation. Also, for several years Jack Gibb had been working with large groups in California that did not rely, as did the La Jolla Program, on previously organized and scheduled small groups. Instead, they were based on non-verbal relationships between participants in order to establish temporary 'communities'.

Further, it should be noted that the British psychiatrist Wilfred Bion had begun serious small group therapy work at the Tavistock Clinic in London before 1948. Then, in 1957, the able and pioneering British educator A. John Allaway (1971), wishing to find a way for his students to gain knowledge 'experientially' or, as the American psychologist and philosopher William James had suggested, 'as acquaintance', planned a project patterned after the T-Groups, held in Bethel, Maine in the United States. Allaway at his University of Leicester and in cooperation with the Tavistock Institute for Human Relations conducted the first British 'Study Groups'.

Using Bion's theory as a basis for the work, these groups evolved through 1968, gradually eliminating activities, such as lectures, that did not provoke learning-from-doing. Following the Americans, who simulated the 'town council', the 'Tavistock Conference' eventually developed into today's well-known large-group activity. At present, these groups may fall short of his goals. Nevertheless, Allaway deserves credit for generalizing the educational nature of the activity from 'training' and 'simulation of town council exercises' toward *learning in an open ambiance of a large group.*

Later, patterned after the La Jolla Program, American entrepreneurs organized European 'cross-cultural communications workshops'. These, again, whether they appeared otherwise or not, enlisted staff members with the expectation of facilitating small-group encounters. Thus, small encounter groups were part of an implicit structure. The plenary sessions had no function other than to be a large-group encounter as opposed to a small-group encounter. In other words, a meeting where one could say what one pleased but the group took no action, one way or another. Later, these plenary sessions would decide *how and when* to divide into small groups for personal encounter, but never *whether* to divide (McIlduff and Coghlan, 1993).

The large group workshop considered here
Departing from these experiments, seventeen-day-long workshops begun in 1973 (Wood, 1984) established the gathering together of the entire 'community' as the core of activities. Thus, conditions were established in order that the workshops should be designed as much as possible by participants themselves. Individually, they established their own tuition fees, commensurate with personal income levels, to pay for the costs of the program (Rogers, Wood, Nelson, Fuchs and Meador, 1986). Once face-to-face in meetings, they formulated the activities and parceled the time for them according to their desires.

Participants were invited as colleagues, not as customers, not as subjects in an experiment, not as students in training, nor as an audience for a conference. They were considered as equals with the organizers, learners in a mutual adventure of discovery. Staff members (including Rogers himself) did not hold themselves apart from community activities. They were involved as full-time participants.

An early intention of these meetings was an attempt to answer, 'How can one function specifically, locally, and privately, in such a way that personal actions would also contribute to the welfare of the community?' (DuBos, 1981).

In this endeavor, the workshops were group-centered. Therefore, the primary function of the organizers was, as agents of the group, to do what it *could not*; that is:

    1. Choose the date and duration of the workshop.

  2. Arrange the place.
  3. State the intention of the event.
  4. Invite participants.

Each of these decisions should not be taken lightly. Each has implications for the others, as well as for the outcome of the event. This will be discussed further later.

Before deciding anything on behalf of the participants, staff members asked themselves, 'Might this decision oppress or empower the person?' The convenors did not wish to make any decisions which might infringe on individual freedom, no matter how trivial the issue might seem (for example, assigning people to living quarters or allowing them to choose for themselves).

Although the organizers determined the beginning, when participants arrived and were finally face-to-face in one room, a group-centered process guided the deliberations. Thus, it was not that there was *no* structure, as some imagine, it was that the staff structured what the group could not and, when face-to-face, they structured the event together as participants.

Naturally, when necessary, the participants would alter staff decisions to conform to the group's needs as they changed. Furthermore, though convenors decided little more than the items listed above in the name of the group, they did not neglect simple initial choices, which if put before the group were likely to throw it into hopeless and chaotic immobility. Thus, instead of presenting participants, tired from sometimes long and arduous journeys, with the possibility of a lengthy and frustrating discussion about whether to 'go out for pizza' or 'send in Chinese', they simply planned the menu for the first few days. Later, the group took over this task.

Doubtless, participants and convenors alike had multiple expectations. They came for personal growth, to alter their style of living, with intentions to benefit humanity, to become effective professionally, to feel good, to see what happens, to overcome the tedium of a dull relationship or unrewarding work, for attention, to have an adventure. Individual intentions were legion. What was important was that participants would agree on a common goal: let's say, 'to explore, through direct experience in a large group, implications of the approach that gave birth to client-centered therapy'. Even though this phrase might have meant something different for each participant, 'We are all in this *together*; let's see what we can accomplish', formed the collective intention.

Organized around a collective intention, the potential for realizing 'community' was also more likely: A person's cries for help might be heard and responded to. Multiplicity in unity might be perceived.

What were the outcomes?
Depending on one's point of view, outcomes have been both positive and negative. Perhaps a more fruitful way to look at this question is not only from the private, but also from the universal perspective.

The private perspective: Could a person's cry for help be heard?
Let us consider these workshops from the point of view of the several criteria that are often mentioned as their justification:
1. Efficacy as *psychotherapy*.
2. Means of enhancing *interpersonal relations*/an environment for *resolving intergroup conflicts* through *integrating conflicting values*.
3. Opportunities for *creative problem solving*.

1. Efficacy as *psychotherapy* (healing by the group, healing of the group)
There have been many anecdotal reports that have supported the belief that workshops were constructive on the basis of a variety of personal criteria. The few researches (Barrett-Lennard, 1977; Bozarth, 1982; Nelson, 1977; Wood, 1994b) that gathered and analyzed written evaluations from individual participants have not disputed this view. However, they have shown that although a few participants felt very good about the experience and very good about themselves afterwards, a few also did *not* feel good and reported disappointing personal experiences. The vast majority (over 90% in the Bozarth study) felt the experience to have been agreeable and regarded the learning as beneficial.

Large-group workshop experiences *can* be, and frequently are, therapeutic for some participants. Previously (Wood, 1982), I have given an example of a person 'breaking down' emotionally and becoming disruptive, threatening the safety of himself and others. Conventional attempts to resolve this crisis having failed, he and the group together, moment by moment, mutually developed a successful course of action. The creative response of the large group bore out Buber's (1958) insight: 'Only when every means has collapsed does the [truly significant] meeting come about' (p.12).

A clear conclusion that may be drawn from the discussion is that these large group workshops could not be considered as 'efficient psychotherapy'. Although the group is capable of acting in a manner that respects the security, well-being and dignity of both itself and the individual, it cannot be considered to help a sufficient number of participants in a psychotherapeutic sense, certainly not to a degree that would offset concerns about the apparently negative effects it may have on some others.

Even when the group *is* therapeutic (which it almost always is for someone), the process is not the same as in individual counseling. The most obvious difference is that the group facilitator (when one has been assigned) rarely has a central role in a participant's personality change. The large group, in this regard, functions very similar to reports of the American group psychotherapist Irvin Yalom's (1985) patients who had successfully completed treatment. When asked about the 'turning point' in their therapy, they invariably recounted an 'incident that is highly laden emotionally and involves some other group member, rarely the therapist'.

Even in a demonstration of individual psychotherapy within a large group workshop, a client may be more influenced by the group itself than by the therapist (Slack, 1985; Rogers, 1985).

2. Means of enhancing *interpersonal relations*/an environment for resolving *intergroup conflicts* through *integrating opposing values*

Conventional psychotherapy is not the only option for satisfying personal and integrative needs in the large group workshop. The group has other ways, some quite complex, to respond to this function.

'Innovative learning' (Botkin, Elmandjra and Malitza, 1979) is that inventiveness that occurs as a reaction to sudden shock, crisis, dangerous scarcity, adversity. It exposes the whole as well as the parts, dealing with multiple causes and effects as well as 'interrelationships between key elements'.[5]

If nothing more urgent than the question of how to organize time (breaking into small groups) or what housekeeping rules to establish (such as, smoking or non-smoking) is on the table, the group will occupy itself with such issues. In general, it will deal with whatever is most urgent. As long as the problems the group faces are real and not contrived, the possibility for resolution, as well as further innovative learning exists.

The following is an example of innovative learning. Carlos, a 12 year-old orphan who lived with a poor family, was not inscribed in the large group workshop. He was staying temporarily with his brother, a handyman employed by the institute which housed the workshop participants.

Some participants had reported that jewelry and small sums of money were missing from their rooms. Carlos was suspected. A woman complained that he was sexually aggressive toward her. 'Something has got to be done about this boy,' several people demanded.

A long and frequently heated discussion ensued. It involved the entire group. On the one side, the list of suspicions of the boy grew. One person said that Carlos made insulting gestures towards her. Another said the kid had a bad face. Someone else reminded the group that thousands of homeless marauders, just Carlos's age, were robbing and murdering citizens in the cities. This group of speakers concluded that the boy was a threat to the security of the community and should be immediately removed.

On the other side, some participants said that they had not found him offensive. He had been courteous with them. He even helped one lady with her luggage when she arrived. They defended his offenses as childlike and innocent, as not meant to be aggressive, merely playful, and unjustly interpreted. They argued that Carlos had no adequate supervision at home and if he remained with the workshop group, at least he would have a chance for a positive experience with responsible people.

Though some saw him as good, others as bad, the group reached the conclusion that its role was not to judge anyone's character. However, it did have a responsibility to decide what to do about participants' strong sentiments surrounding the lad and what course of action to take regarding his presence.

A few people observed that Carlos was, in fact, a member of the community and that the fair course of action would be to consult him in any decision that affected him. 'We are a family,' someone finally suggested. Around this metaphor participants were able to rally and integrate their conflicting values. It was agreed that those who felt more intensely (both for and against Carlos's presence in the workshop) would put the group's concerns before him. They would discuss with him how they felt, find out how he felt, and try to find some solution they thought would work to everyone's satisfaction.[6]

In the meeting, Carlos said that he did not realize his behavior was frightening anyone. He was acting in his accustomed way. When he realized others felt threatened, he was willing to change. Also, he wished to participate in the workshop. He wanted to study dance with Grace; to learn massage with Laura; with Clare, to learn music and art; and with his brother, to learn to drive a car. They all agreed. He agreed to conform to the behavior which governed all participants.

Carlos stayed in the workshop. He not only abided by the consensual rules, but became an exemplary citizen. Those who previously feared him became his friends. Those who initially supported his point of view were not disappointed. In the end he made one of the more pointed observations of the group, 'This year there was lot of drama and not much adventure. I expect that next time there will be more adventure and less drama.'

• Integrating conflicting values
Every person in the community was involved in the decision-making process, including Carlos. People showed respect for each other's feelings. They were honest: their statements matched their thoughts and sentiments. They respected the dignity of each member of the community, even a 12-year-old who was not even officially registered in the workshop. And, this participation included an intention to cooperate and use dialogue to reach an intelligent solution.

In the example above, a clash of values was what really seemed at stake:
'A citizen has a right to live free from threat.'
'The group has a responsibility to protect its members and to govern the behavior of its members.'
'The individual should be free to act differently and still be accepted. We should not have to conform to someone else's opinions of proper behavior.'
'The community is responsible for looking after its children.'
'We should be governed by humane feelings, not by cold rules.'
'Security is more important than anyone's feelings. If people are concerned about the boy's feelings, that's their problem, not mine.'
'If any member of the group has a problem, it is the whole group's problem.'

In many conflicts that arise thusly, I can say, 'Yes,' to each side in the conflict. When I heard the members of the community call for greater security, I said to myself, 'Yes, I want security.' When I heard their opponents call for greater respect for the individual, even if it is a 12-year-old, I said, 'Yes, let's respect the lad. Give him a chance.' Why could we not have security *and* respect the individual?

The group strived for the best and surrendered to the better. Within the metaphor of 'family', a range of conflicting values was accepted. A person who favored the boy, perceived him as someone to help to improve. One who was skeptical of the boy's trustworthiness, after accepting him as part of the 'family', saw him as someone who was merely different from the run of the mill. Using a metaphor to make an idea clearer is thought to tend to convince, not on the basis of the idea's merits but, due to the familiarity of the metaphor (Bowers and Osborn, 1966).

3. Opportunities for *creative problem solving* (the culture and the individual transformed)
• What is culture?
Through biological evolution (that is, natural selection) our organisms have evolved instincts, needs, dispositions, that is, a human nature. Culture consists of additionally acquired behaviors and thought that satisfy the biological and psychological demands of human nature through individuals in a given group (Harris, 1989).

Natural selection takes thousands of years to bring about significant changes in an organism. Culture may change rapidly through attaining a different perspective, a new organizing idea, a new value. However, changes in a culture may not necessarily be beneficial for the biological evolution of the species. Also, it is difficult to know what changes to 'select'. Though 'conscious change' may not be easy, achieving the goal of conscious collective intention is not impossible.

• A large group workshop culture transformed by interactive dialogue
A participant confronted members of the group with a furious need to 'stage a happening'. Other participants were eager at first to support what he had proposed as a theatrical 'play'.

Although the protagonist's proposal seemed in agreement with the established group culture, many had reservations. They feared some kind of violence. In the subsequent intensely emotional encounter to clarify his intentions and alleviate their fears, a prolonged drama was lived by all. By the end of the afternoon, he announced, after deep reflection, 'I have realized something already. It has been enough. It is complete. I have got what I need, not necessarily what I had been seeking, what I thought I would need. This is it. I am grateful.'

The man followed his desire to understand himself and it took him in a surprising direction – not toward violence but away from it. Perhaps, just as other large group workshops had, this community could have handled the crisis of an 'emotional breakdown', if he had become a 'problem'. This group, however, demanded more. Participants were sensitive to the pattern of their 'community' life and its consequences to the person. In a sense, they empathically 'lived' the experience. He changed and the group changed together with him (Wood, 1984).

In fact, the very culture of the workshop had been revised. The British philosopher Mary Midgley (1978) has observed that we could not have survived as a species were we not able to be conditioned. By the same token, changing the culture, is perhaps as natural a function as adapting to it. She states, 'When people resist and change the culture they were brought up with, they do so because their nature demands it. Conditioning fails here, because that which was conditioned is stronger than its conditioning'.

The universal perspective: Did unity emerge?
• The effect of unity

Many people become very nervous with talk of 'the group'. A psychologist friend of mine once said, 'What makes me uneasy about collectives is the realization that they don't make statements or interpret positions; only individuals do that.'

I agree with him. *And* I think it should be remembered that although collectives do not interpret positions, they do *create* them, the same way they make statements, by their actions. Although the group may not be an 'organism' (at least not in the strict biological sense), it is doubtless reality. For example, the United States Supreme Court has ruled, based on statistical analysis of racial distribution of employees in the organization, that a black former employee was discriminated against. Although no single individual was found to have been discriminatory, the *group* had discriminated against the individual (Time Magazine, July 11, 1988, p. 13).

To draw attention to collective difficulties, the Danish philosopher Soren Kierkegaard is widely quoted as saying, 'The crowd is untruth'. (My friend quotes him also.) Martin Buber's (1957) reply is more precise, 'I do not know if Kierkegaard is right when he says that the crowd is untruth – I should rather describe it as non-truth since (in distinction from some of its masters) it is not in the least opposed to it'. Any warning against the group, Buber urged, can be only a preface to 'the true question to the single one'. Thus, except in specific cases where it is deserved, throwing the blame on either the individual or the group does not seem constructive.

• The perception of unity

For the individual to be aware of the group as a whole is not merely an intellectual process. It involves a different way of seeing, using the mind as an organ of perception, not merely as a computer or an arbitrator. This way of seeing is often related (though not restricted) to artistic expression. The French painter Paul Cézanne, for example, said, 'The landscape thinks itself in me and I am its consciousness' (Merleau-Ponty, 1964). Similarly, one might say that the group 'thinks itself' in the participant, allowing for global understandings.

In large groups, the properties of the whole come through the individual. As Bortoft (1996) has written, illuminating the thought of the German philosopher Martin Heidegger, 'The part [individual] is a place for "presencing" the whole'. Thus, the individual is not accidental. He or she is *special*, in that the whole is shown through the individual. The whole is not a *thing*. As Bortoft emphasizes, it is more an 'active absence', emerging simultaneously with the accumulation of parts because it is *immanent* within them.

This extremely important potential of the group should perhaps be accompanied by a warning announcement. Perceiving the unity, without participants – at the same time – maintaining an adequate awareness of their personal reality, can result in 'epidemic' emotions. These may be harmful, at worst; simply a waste of time, at best. The danger of becoming overly fascinated with 'group' and losing sight of the individual, has been observed – not only in flamboyant cults – but also in otherwise constructive activities. For example, there is evidence from Tavistock-type groups to suggest that *emphasizing* the group-as-a-whole, *without* attention to the constructive experience of individual members and without an ambiance which includes empathy and acceptance may not only be unhelpful, but even harmful to participants (Colson and Horwitz, 1983).

• More on unity
Nevertheless, the perception of unity – or better, the perception of the multiplicity in unity, may be immensely useful. Unity according to Goethe, is organized by consciousness. What is consciousness? Bortoft (1996), describing Goethe's perspective, states that, ' Consciousness has the structure of intentionality – it would be better to say that consciousness *is* intentionality'. He says that, with regard to the intuitive knowledge of nature, 'when the phenomenon becomes its own theory, we have the ontological condition that the knower and the known constitute an indivisible whole'. That is, a unity.

Thus, this knowing, what we are considering here as 'unity,' is 'an evolutionary development of the phenomenon and not just a subjective activity of the mind'. (Bortoft, 1996).

• Time out for theoretical speculation
The face-to-face, existential, large group is very old – from the beginnings of humanity. It involves various rituals which, though perhaps in different forms, still exist in present-day groupings.

The group and its rituals were important even before the appearance of *homo sapiens sapiens*. Monkeys spent (and spend) some 20% of their time grooming one another. The act of picking leaves, dried hairs, ticks and fleas from each other's coats forms influential alliances. In addition to maintaining personal hygiene, the practice induces a state of relaxation, a lowering of heart-rate and a reduction of signs of stress in participants. At the same time, participants are observing group life: who is doing what? To whom? Who is free-loading? Pulling more than his or her weight? Who is advertising what?

Dunbar (1996) thinks that language developed from early contact-calls to facilitate bonding. Gossip – which is social grooming – took the place of physical grooming in large groups. Language was needed to keep track of all that was going on within a large number of individuals. Language, in addition to facilitating 'bonding and networking', in the current jargon, has evidently also been used to formalize and manage rituals as well.

Personal opinions, preferences, experiences, thoughts, feelings. These are the fuel of two-thirds of everyday conversation and most of all large group dialogue. In a large group workshop, through dialogue, participants express personal opinions, emotions, feelings, concerns, theories, regarding themselves and others. They clash in conversations over values, line up behind 'issues', and generally try to figure out who they are in this situation.

However, there are still other considerations. Large groups have affected consciousness itself. The British archeologist Steven Mithen (1996) thinks that in the development of general-purpose language from social language, 'consciousness adopted the role of an integrating mechanism for knowledge previously "trapped" in separate specialized intelligences' in the mind. Thus, consciousness becomes a serious consideration, not only in evolutionary theory, but in understanding *the phenomenon of large groups.*

As with physical grooming, during social grooming, by virtue of merely being together, a unique state of consciousness is induced in participants. Thus, frequently without their total awareness, participants are in 'exceptional states of consciousness' (James, 1896) in which what would be contradictory thoughts or perceptions in the 'generalized reality orientation' (Shor, 1959) may coexist in a person's mind, allowing for creative solutions to problems that would not be possible under everyday circumstances. This state is likened to that of playing a musical instrument where, 'The normal self is not excluded from conscious participation in the performance, though initiative seems to come from elsewhere' (James, 1890).

Contradictory states of consciousness, such as exerting autonomy, on the one hand, and surrendering to the group thought, on the other, may co-exist. Neither loss of autonomy, nor lack of contribution in an integrative effort results. The unity, which has, to this point, remained vague, begins to be tangible. A perceivable 'it' provides guidance for those who have the keenness of sensibility to follow. The 'it' can become a context in which members may assemble the relevant parts of their own consciousness both to give themselves a clearer personal definition *and* an integrated relation to the purpose or meaning of the group.

Such perceptions may be more difficult to describe than to realize. The best description I have seen for such phenomena is that of Bortoft (1996). He states, 'When we see the intrinsic connections, the phenomenon is experienced as a whole, and it is part of this experience that we recognize the wholeness of the phenomenon to be part of the phenomenon itself and not added to it by the mind – even though it is experienced through the mind instead of the senses. ... We have both together: the separation and the wholeness.'

In the previous example of *group innovative learning*, this unity was being pursued. In the example of *the culture and the individual transformed*, the participants were, for the most part, focused on this unity. Thus, conflicting values were integrated in reality, if not in words.

• Anticipating the future (intuitive self-government)
Reaching a point of harmony and clear communications between participants is

often referred to as 'building community'. In the beginning of a large group workshop a committee of participants made a proposal for organizing meeting-times and activities for the first few days. Discussion of this plan, which at first was enthusiastically accepted by the majority, eventually led to abandoning the plan in favor of participants 'following their intuition'. Amazingly, participants *were* able to be aware of not only their individual patterns of behavior but also a pattern suggested by the 'group as a whole'. A private impulse (from the individual's point of view), shared by many, sent people to the meeting room at the same time. Participants could organize their activities 'intuitively' (Wood, 1984).

• Going beyond democracy: Participatory intuition
In another workshop (Wood, 1984), a lengthy debate about whether or not to take a 'day off' from the emotional intensity of regular meetings ended without resolution. A few days passed and participants spontaneously turned to leisure activities and no meetings were held. No plan was made, decision stated or vote taken. Not policy, but collective intention guided the group. The act, though spontaneous, was not impulsive. It was intelligent, but not strictly logical. It was a democratic process that did not resort to the compromise of voting. It seemed to represent what the American sociologist Ernest Becker (1969) called, 'An anchoring of power in as many subjectivities as there are those who fashion it'.

Quite often a conclusion is not spoken nor explicitly acknowledged. It is an aspect of non-verbal behavior and, as the American anthropologist Edward Hall (l959) has observed, it is 'in accordance with an elaborate and secret code that is written nowhere, known by no one, and understood by all'.

Sometimes a clever person will ask the group, just before adjourning, for a show of hands as to who agrees with and who does not agree with the 'decision' that has been taken tacitly. When hands are raised, the group is divided as in the beginning. Two minds are apparent. One (non-verbal) has decided on a consensual course of action. The other (voting) maintains its opinion unchanged.

Notable failures
In a recent article (Wood, 1997), I have defined what I take to be an 'effective large group workshop'. In this present chapter, I have also tried to present conditions that might lead up to such an event. My suggestions seem to me to be necessary, but not sufficient. Without considering hundreds which were not, in some 16 workshops that were carefully conceived and organized, only four would be judged effective by the criteria I have established. Though not nearly exhaustive, I would like to mention some of the reasons, in my opinion, that some were not effective.

Bad will
• The individual is satisfied; the group, not
In most large group workshops substantial individual learning will take place, but innovative group learning is more doubtful and easily obstructed. In the United

States, for example, a workshop was conducted in which a legal activist was present. In the group meetings he put forth (like other participants) his opinion. However, unlike others, he insisted on a point of view which was *consistently contrary* to any consensus which began to emerge.

This crusade, he eventually admitted, was a 'test' to see if the group could 'tolerate diversity'.

From my experience, innovative learning *needs* the expression of genuine diversity to find creative solutions. What it cannot tolerate, as this fellow proved, is consistent bad will. Following the unity in the group is a subtle cooperative venture. The group could stand diversity, but without this man's constructive participation no integrated solution could be found. Diversity was plentiful. What was missing, and was impossible under the circumstances, was creative integration.

The American sociologist Leonard Doob and his associates (1970), in a workshop using the National Training Laboratories approach to try to resolve a border dispute between three African states, encountered similar effects of bad will. The organizers reported that a participant's 'calculatedly disruptive behavior' frequently manifested itself 'most when some progress or agreement was close at hand'.

• An appearance of unity

In another workshop, a participant arrogantly announced that he intended to tape-record the meetings. Some participants accepted his proposal. Those who objected, he tried to bully into conformity. The objectors also held stubbornly to their feelings. A long discussion ensued. No decision was reached, but he apparently willingly withdrew his request to tape-record.

It seemed, at the time, a true group decision. However, later it was noticed that the man had sulked through the remainder of the workshop. In this case, the experience of one participant was not satisfactory. He did not show the necessary *humility* to abandon his motives for a mutual solution (which may have even satisfied his real desire). Other members of the group did not show the necessary *autonomy* to reopen the problem when they saw that he had become alienated from the group.

Falsely assuming that previous successful experience automatically applies in a new situation

In 1977, I first came to Brazil with other members of the Center for Studies of the Person in La Jolla to convene a large group workshop similar to those we had initiated in the U.S.A. in 1974. As a prelude to this workshop which would be held in the State of Rio de Janeiro with some 300 participants, we also convened even larger two-day workshops in three major Brazilian cities: Recife, São Paulo and Rio de Janeiro.

We began in Recife, with a meeting in a gigantic sports complex. The area was arranged for a traditional academic presentation: rows of movable chairs lined up in front of a stage with a long table at which the presenters sat before microphones.

Other microphones on long extension cords had been provided for members of the audience to ask questions. There were said to be some 800 to 1,000 participants.

Our plan was for each of the Americans to give a brief talk on our own interests and then to invite discussion from the audience. After only a few minutes, the lecture became tedious. Members of the audience complained that they wanted to participate.

With some misgivings, we eventually formed one large circle. We would converse. Microphones were passed hand-to-hand to whoever wished to speak. At first, the preachers took the floor: A Christian padre from the interior, a syndicate boss, a marxist sociology professor. Familiar rhetoric.

Perhaps what characterized the conversation in the remaining hours was this statement: 'This is the first time I have stood up in public and said what I feel . . . to criticize, to say what I really think.' And this: 'I haven't said anything until now, but I just have to express my joy. . . . I came here feeling so lost, like I was alone in my pain and my struggle. It's all just too big for me: the poverty of my people, the political realities of the world in which I live, the pain in my marriage, my family, my job. I couldn't do it alone . . . and now I realize that I am not facing it alone. . . . I feel strong, I feel nourished and now I can go on. Maybe this won't last, but in a way that doesn't really matter. What matters to me is that I feel it today'. (Bowen, Miller, Rogers and Wood, 1979).

For us, this was a grand success: more than 800 persons could speak in one meaningful conversation.

Next, we went to São Paulo where the large group meeting was held in a high-tech auditorium with fixed seats in tiers. Never mind, we thought. The space is not important (a mistaken belief from client-centered therapy where the space was rigidly controlled: two people in a closed room). The important thing is that people be able to speak personally (a mistaken generalization from our previous success). We know how to do this work. Weren't we effective in Recife? (A genuine success, but under different conditions.) Our experience has taught us that all you have to do is provide the 'opportunity' for people to converse. (However, we had not yet learned the full meaning of 'opportunity'.)

We Americans stationed ourselves in various parts of the auditorium facing the empty stage. Microphones were available on long cords. Rogers invited people to speak.

The outcome was a disaster. A colossal failure. Listeners looked at the backs of others, while the anonymous speaker's voice came as if from the clouds as it issued from the speakers on the stage. In the chaos, many people walked out and apparently never returned.

That night Rogers captured the 'living with uncertainty' nature of such activities when he wrote in his journal:

'Either I had helped launch an incredibly stupid experiment, doomed to failure, or I had helped to innovate a whole new way of permitting 800 people to sense their own potentialities and to participate in forming their own learning experience. There was no way to predict which it would prove to be'.

The morning newspaper printed its opinion. The headline read something like: *Psicólogo Faz Nada: Provoca Caos* (Psychologist does nothing: provokes chaos). Our Brazilian friends began to needle us about 'Caos Rogers', instead of Carl Rogers.

What went wrong?

First, instead of respecting the culture and meeting people 'where they are', we imposed our values and desires upon them. Had we respected the culture, perhaps we would have favored the traditional beginning: on stage, short talks, questions and answers, asking for and following participants' suggestions as to how to proceed, perhaps breaking into small groups and finally a grand plenary conversation – which is what happened on the second day.

Second, we ignored the extremely important influence of the environment. Ignorantly, we thought we could overcome ambiental constraints with our 'principle' of person-to-person encounter.

Finally, and perhaps most devastating, we did not face this new situation as new, but tried to apply our latest 'learnings' to an event that had still more to teach us.

On the final leg of our trip, in Rio de Janeiro, we started over from scratch, though a bit wiser. We paid attention to the environment, arranging for movable chairs to be placed in a large conference room. This was not done in order to form a circle. It was done in order to *have the option*, should the group decide it wished to form a circle and speak in one conversation. We proceeded step by step, involving the entire group in every act. In this sense, the eventual success in Rio (which duplicated that in Recife) was more significant because it involved an 'informed intention'.

Pitfalls in 'modeling' an application, instead of seeking a creative experience together
In 1985, the Rust Workshop in Austria was an attempt to contribute to conflict resolution in 'The Central American Challenge', Rogers (1986) relates that 'Among the 50 participants were high-level government officials, especially from Central America, and other leading political and professional figures, from seventeen countries in all'.

From Rogers's own reports and comments of his staff:
- the facilitators remained aloof from the participants,
- because of ignorance, the facilitators sometimes offended members of other cultures,
- the facilitators tried to impose their own cultural values on participants,
- there was 'inadequate communication and inadequate understanding', between the facilitators and the Latin-Americans who were more intensely involved in trying to resolve disputes in their region.

Rogers's (1984) central hypothesis for groups was that, 'groups of individuals have within themselves vast resources for understanding and accepting their dynamics, for reduction and resolution of conflicts, and for constructive change in group goals and behavior'. This perspective supposedly guided the workshop.

Nevertheless, in this workshop there was something like one 'facilitator' for every three 'participants'. The organizers' behavior hardly showed much confidence in the group's ability to organize itself constructively.

Also, partitioning the time for small groups, big groups, lectures and so forth, further suggests the organizers distrusted the group's abilities to deal appropriately with its own urgencies.

The real problem of this workshop was that its *primary intention was not even conflict resolution*. Rogers (1984) in the workshop proposal states that, 'The purpose of this workshop will be threefold. [First], it will give the participants the opportunity to experience a person-centered approach to group facilitation to the reduction of whatever tensions exist or arise in the participant group'. To have as a *primary* goal, wanting to *give* people an experience of the person-centered approach, not only is contrary to the approach itself (which might more likely adopt an objective such as, 'to facilitate the exploration of conflict'), it nearly guarantees failure.

And, there is evidence that the group was not effective, even on the personal level. One of the most important Latin American dignitaries, influential in organizing the event from Central America, reportedly left the workshop 'feeling hurt and somewhat unrecognized' (Wood, 1994a).

Of course, in spite of these or other problems, it is likely that some people considered this a significant experience. That participants have different (even opposing) opinions and perceptions is not uncommon in large group workshops. The point is that a common thread is needed (either one present from the beginning through collective conscious intention or one created from urgency during the encounter) to allow the possibility to use these differences, even differences in values, to find creative solutions.

By respecting the inherent creative potential in any group and beginning with the attitude, 'Let's see what we can accomplish together, applying all our will and resources', and genuinely being willing to be changed by what occurs, organizers at least begin with the potential for an effective workshop.

Squandering human potential: Becoming a (religious) sub-culture, instead of fostering learning
There are several annual and bi-annual large group encounters currently being held. The longest running of this type was the European cross-cultural communications workshops. This model persisted for some 20 years.

Although these events were doubtless useful for many individuals – for personal growth or for political reasons – they have never to my knowledge shown significant evidence of improving cross-cultural communications, nor of being effective, as I have defined effectiveness. These workshops were largely emotional 'happenings', whose main function was reproducing themselves.

The most interesting aspect – though I do not know if it should be considered constructive – is that such on-going workshops tend to create their own culture.

• Cross-cultural communications workshop culture
Since there were apparently no restrictions on participation in these European workshops, a great many people made a habit of attending year after year (McIlduff and Coghlan, 1993). This familial population both created and preserved a specific culture. 'Typically, at the beginning of a large group workshop', those who have participated, facilitated and organized cross-cultural communication workshops write, 'some participants speak of their experience of others who are already familiar with the "group culture", who know "the rules", the correct way to speak in order to be given attention' (MacMillan and Lago, 1993, p. 26).

The significant cultural differences that may have existed between participants were effectively neutralized in the meetings by the influence of the workshop culture itself. In considering a list of activities and conventions, suggested by Hall (1959, 1966), that differ between cultures, virtually every one (verbal communication, comfort distance between people, appointment times, odors, conventions for discussion, establishing acquaintances) is determined by the *workshop culture* and not by the native cultures of participants.

The most discussed *tradition* in these workshops (McIlduff and Coghlan, 1993) is the activity called 'fragmenting into small groups'. The consistency of this phenomenon is suggested in these statements: 'Despite an overall attendance of more than 3000 participants, the workshops have developed a fairly predictable pattern . . .' and, 'The "community" spends considerable time discussing the merits of moving into smaller groups, facilitated by the (at times, rather intimidatingly large) staff that has been assembled for this purpose'.

The relation between this tradition and the organizers' intentions is touched on by the British counseling psychologist Colin Lago, who has been a keen observer of cross-cultural communication workshops. He suggests that the staff group may unwittingly influence the group process solely through its constitution. Lago (1994) states, 'It could be argued that the culture of the staff team, already dominated by English and staffed by sophisticated travelers, joined together in their person-centered philosophies and working practices, successfully over-rode concerns about cultural identity, cultural understanding and patterns of culturally determined behavior'.

This ritual or stylized behavior often has the effect of preventing an effective group and thus squandering human potential. One 'first time participant' observed, 'Some experienced large group talkers were doing their thing or performing their ballet dance. It did not encourage me to trust them. Rather, I thought I witnessed people's needs becoming at times so overwhelming that they burst forth irrespective of the level of comfort or ease or trust that they felt towards the group'.

Another participant related that she had joined the workshop to discuss certain issues. She was disappointed that her ideas, opinions and views were not given the same weight as others' feelings. 'Why do feelings come before these things?' she demanded to know. 'It seems that there is a tyranny of feelings here' (McIlduff and Coghlan, 1989, p. 81).

What conditions may figure in the formation of an effective large group workshop?

Even when evaluating large group workshops on a careful and rational basis, it is still not easy to judge their value. As we have seen, they may be psychotherapeutic, but not psychotherapy. They are capable of innovative learning. But, when this innovation is 'modeled', it may be ineffective. They may be laboratories to learn how culture is formed and transformed. But when they go on for a time, they tend to create their own culture, perhaps become a religion. They may organize themselves intuitively. But when people set out to 'follow the intuitive wisdom of the group', they may create superstitions at best, chaos at worst. Large group meetings are capable of delicate consensual decisions. But if only one participant has bad will, multiplicity remains without unity.

These statements may be true for any group. We know that practically any conference or encounter will produce constructive experiences for some participants. Likewise, in some religious and similar services, unity may be achieved. To be effective, the large group workshop must achieve both. Thus, it is worthwhile to study what conditions may contribute to effectivity.

Impressions from an initial large-group experience

A first-time participant in a recent large group workshop thought it was unique because there was no power structure established beforehand, to dictate participants' daily behavior. There were no 'facilitators' or specialists of any kind to guide participants, to 'help' them understand their experience, help them to 'communicate', or to 'organize'. For this person, this represented a 'real liberty'. The 'space' of the group was open to everyone, as she perceived. And, she felt she had as much 'power' as anyone else – 'old-timer' or 'newcomer'. The strength of one's voice depended on the purity of expression, not on the intended effect, nor the familiarity of the slogans issued, nor from whose mouth it was emitted.

She was also impressed that there were no pre-established rules, not even 'norms' of behavior that she could perceive. Of course, there existed the deep-seated cultural habits that each brought, but the main objectives of the group and the values that governed them seemed to be formed largely through dialogue.

The 'plasticity' of the group was impressive. The group seemed to be what the participants, collectively, made of it. The direction seemed to be in each one's hands. Each was responsible. The sensation of equality and consideration for the best in each one, in regard to his or her 'standing' in the community was also felt to be unique (Freire, 1997).

Another one-time participant, an American clinical psychologist, is ambivalent about the value of large group workshops. He fails to see the value of such endeavors, in spite of his significant personal learning. Reporting on his experience of 20 years ago, he relates a significant impact on his life. He learned to speak when he genuinely had something to say, as opposed to merely 'getting airtime'. 'When I spoke from those moments of strong feeling,' he recently reports, 'my communications were inevitably clear, meaningful and impactful. I still rely on this learning'.

Behind the scenes: Conscious intention

The large group workshop begins when the organizers decide that they will convene it and it will have such-and-such a purpose. Their values, beliefs, intentions contribute to the constitution of the workshop by providing an 'organizing idea'.

Thus their values are not incidental. They shape the initial structure of the event. The organizers' opinions about how others should be provided for, welcomed, treated, will be expressed in their preparations. Qualities they respect, they will look for in others. Nevertheless, in the composition of the group, they will likely want diversity. They will wish for mutual respect between persons, will expect people to fight for their own unique point of view, but give it up for a perspective that will be more creative in helping the group resolve a conflict, solve a problem, learn together.

They choose the *dates* for the event. A time that is convenient for themselves and also for what they imagine would be convenient for participants. The goal of the workshop may also effect the dates chosen. Seasons, the lunar cycle, and other factors should be studied for relevance in this choice.

Then, a *place* is chosen based on knowledge of the effects of ambiance on the consciousness of human beings, including the role of space itself (Mintz, 1956; Barker, 1968), the effects of sunshine (Rosenthal, et al., 1984), of air ions (Kreuger and Reed, 1976), low-frequency magnetic fields (Brodeur, 1989) and other 'hidden factors' in creative human processes.

Next, a statement of *intention* is made which reflects all of these considerations. Finally, invitations are issued to applicants who the organizers believe share their intentions sufficiently to create the possibility for an effective large group workshop.

Collective intentionality

Intentions must be chosen and stated carefully so as to 'aim' the workshop in a constructive direction from the start. No matter how one may wish for a self-directed and creative workshop, the introduction of conflicting expectations can derail this course.

For example, in a recent carefully organized large group workshop, the organizers stated simply and precisely the intention for a group-centered meeting to be governed solely by its own necessities. However, inasmuch as the workshop would be held in a place of natural beauty, it was mentioned that certain tourist possibilities might be possible *if* a mid-week break occurred in deliberations. Though merely mentioning a possibility, unwittingly contradictory intentions had been established in a substantial number of participants. One: the group would govern its own course, based on its moment-to-moment needs. And, two: a day off for tourism would occur at mid-week.

As the expected day approached, many people began to discuss tourist plans. Since the topic of these discussions conflicted with what had been taking place in the group, they established a parallel dialogue. The face-to-face, emerging 'life' of the group ran parallel courses: one, seeking the elusive unity of the group; the other, seeking to satisfy previously established desires.

Since many people were equally divided between these two alternatives, the conflict was awkwardly resolved. A day off was taken. Although this amounted to a disruption of the emergence of a unity, a subtle 'it', that had been forming, it was not at all a disappointment, when judged as daily experience. The sight seeing groups reported very satisfying experiences; as did those who remained at the workshop site. In other words, the group *did* deal with its necessities in the most creative way possible under the circumstances. The point is, that had the organizers communicated a less ambiguous intention, a day for tourism might have come about more in harmony with the pace of the total group.

In every stage of development of the workshop, the organizers are agents of the group. Their job is to do what the group *cannot* do for itself. When the participants are finally face-to-face, organizers are no longer needed, as the group can now direct itself.

When people join the 'group', saying 'Yes' to the organizers' intentions, they begin to influence the workshop, with both an 'I' intentionality and a 'We' intentionality.

The American philosopher John Searles, whose thoughts on language and dialogue may also prove relevant to the study of large groups, has asserted that, 'Collective intentionality is a biologically primitive phenomenon that cannot be reduced to, or eliminated in favor of, something else. Every attempt at reducing "We intentionality" to "I intentionality" that I have seen is subject to counterexamples.' He explains, 'There is a big difference between two violinists playing in an orchestra ["We intentionality"], on the one hand, and on the other hand, discovering, while I am practicing my part ["I intentionality"] that someone else in the next room is practicing her part, and thus discovering that, by chance, we are playing some piece in a synchronized fashion' (Searles, 1995). Again, the sum of the parts do not make up a whole. The whole becomes evident in its parts.

When Rogers (1980) perceiving profoundly his client as a unique person also perceived 'what is universally true', it was because the individual was the place for 'presencing' the whole, not a generalization arrived at by seeing many instances. Although Rogers succeeded in this realization, many counselors do not, since they continue to look for a unity in multiplicity instead of the multiplicity in unity.

Implications for the future

What one hears most about implications of such large group workshops as described here is that they could become a device for dealing with future problems. The reasoning often suggests that facilitators could be trained to intervene in large groups and resolve intergroup conflicts, and so forth.

There are two problems with this train of thought.

First, utopian schemes are rarely successful. Radical attempts to engineer a new society have most often been disastrous.

Second, although groups do possess the creativity to deal with unforeseen problems, to prepare interventionists for what they think the future will be like is inevitably to be unprepared. The future almost always holds surprises.

Cultural formation: Following what we are creating

What do people do in large group meetings?

They converse. They tell each other how they feel in the moment, how they see the world, their values, their problems, their opinions, what they regard as 'truths'. Inevitably, personalities and values clash. With good intentions and time a unity may emerge. What should be asked is, 'How does this come about?'

It has been noticed that people in a group speak not merely to those in their immediate vicinity, but also to a 'universal audience'. In the dialogue, there is already an 'it' they unite with (Perelman and Olbrechts-Tyeca, 1969).

Considered in this light, one implication of large group workshops would be a case of Goethe's observation that *the state of 'being known' is a further evolutionary stage of the phenomenon itself* (Bortoft, 1996).

Perhaps by knowing itself, through dialogue, the human grouping may be evolving a creative capacity to deal with its necessities. In organizing a series of large group workshops, between 1974 and 1980, it was frequently noticed that each year's group (which consisted of different individuals) seemed to begin, in terms of its interests, goals, challenges, and its ability to deal with them, where the last group left off. That is, there was a noticeable evolution of learning, from one generation to the next – even though almost all the individuals were different.

This observation may be merely self-deception on the part of the organizers. But, since this hypothesis yields little advancement in knowledge, the hypothesis of *formative causation* might be given serious thought in studying implications of large group workshops.

The hypothesis of formative causation

The British plant physiologist Rupert Sheldrake (1981) has proposed the hypothesis of formative causation to account for such observations that subsequent workshops (separated by time and space with different participants) would seem to know what the earlier groups had previously learned. The hypothesis proposes that 'morphogenetic fields [analogous to other fields in physics] play a causal role in the development and maintenance of the forms of systems at all levels of complexity'. *Formative causation*, although not energetic itself nor reducible to known physical fields, supposedly imposes a spatial order on changes brought about by physical causation. It is likened to a blueprint that, though not energetic, *causes* the specific form of the house. It is not the only cause and without materials, builders, and tools, the house would not come into being.

Preserving human potential

The large group workshop may be a means for preserving the human potential for innovative learning. If the power, wisdom, creativity, whatever constructive outcome the group derives, comes from (the evolutionary quality of) *being together*, without over-controlling leaders, rules of behavior, superstitions, then, simply convening carefully organized groups, with a sensitivity for learning, may preserve human potential.

Not only would participants be learning how to 'exercise personal power', they would, more importantly, be anticipating the future, going beyond democracy with a participatory intuition, finding the healing capacity of the group, learning how culture was formed and transformed. In this and more, they would be cultivating skills (a 'way to be', perhaps) that might be useful in the future as well.

In my pastures, there are dozens of different plants, not one. The unity of Nature includes diversity. One might say that Nature values variety. It preserves potential. A sudden prairie fire (as I have witnessed) will eliminate many promising experiments. However, the unity will persist. Seeds, kept in reserve, will sprout. The pasture's continuity is guaranteed, as is the existence of those who depend on it.

Preserving human potential may be somewhat similar. If the pathways are not blocked by mental or bureaucratic structures, the right person needed by the group at the right time may step forward to provide the necessary leadership, insight, healing. Human capacities may also be cultivated. People may learn to tolerate uncertainty while immersed in mystery, awaiting with anticipation relevant facts in order to act intelligently. Or, one may fiercely fight for a personal point of view, then quickly surrender it for a more inclusive perspective that benefits both the individual and the community. The childish dichotomy between thinking and feeling gives way to turning the best part of oneself toward the best part of another so that something of inestimable value might take place, that neither could have imagined, let alone have produced alone. As the French-American biochemist René DuBos (1981) has observed, 'Nature is not efficient. It is redundant. It always uses things in many different ways, a number of them awkward, rather than aiming first at perfect solutions'.

The aim of this growing knowledge would be Goethe's, 'that through the contemplation of an ever creating nature, we should make ourselves worthy of spiritual participation in her production' (Bortoft, 1996).

Notes

1. On the subject of the evaluation of large group workshops, see Wood (1997). For a discussion of the variables in large group workshops and some of the factors that may be involved in effectivity, see Wood (1984).
2. Although they are excellent for passing information rapidly and inexpensively between people, electronic networks are not yet (and may never be) 'large groups', as discussed in this chapter. In spite of hundreds of 'participants', their relationships are peculiar. A new category of social aggressiveness is being formed around the concept of 'net-rage' (Dunbar, 1996), the tendency to become furious because one's words or intentions are misinterpreted by other correspondents who launch their own private armadas against expressions that may have been used incidentally. This suggests that we have not learned how to be and how to see with regard to this phenomenon which is worthy of careful study.
3. Present-day hunter-gatherer groups camping for the night are said to consist of 30–35 people. Groups who all share the same language (that is, tribes) are said to number 1500–2000.

Studies of primate groupings have revealed a predictable relation between the group size and the animal's neocortex ratio (the volume of the neocortex divided by the volume of the rest of the brain). This suggests that group size may have evolutionary significance. When the human neocortex ratio of 4:1 is plotted on the curve drawn with the above data, a group size of 150 persons is predicted. Large group workshops have been convened with participants numbering in all three of these ranges: 30, 1000, and 150. Each could be said to have a unique 'personality', but the indices of effectivity would have been similar.

Of additional interest are reports that excavations of the earliest farming villages in the Near East (around 5000 BC) have suggested that the inhabitants numbered around 150. This also happens to be the figure for villages of horticulturists of our day, in the Philippines, Indonesia, and South America.

Striking similarities between this kind of village life and an effective large group workshop comes from a film produced by the Brazilian cinematographer Joaquim Assis, *Ô Gente, Pois Não*. Documenting life in a horticulturist-size village in north-eastern Brazil, it illustrates almost every feature of an effective large group workshop. It is a mistake to interpret this evidence for a 'back to nature' movement. It is more valuable as evidence that human groupings already have within them a being-together wisdom which, if not interfered with, may serve the necessities of the group and the species.

4. As far as I know, the first time Rogers used this concept in print was in a journal article when he referred to 'person-centeredness' (Rogers, 1955).

5. 'Innovative learning' is opposed to 'maintenance learning' which is 'the acquisition of fixed outlooks, methods, and rules for dealing with known and recurring situations ... the type of learning designed to maintain an existing system or established way of life'. Maintenance learning is essential to the continuation of much of civilization's infrastructure (Botkin, Elmandjra and Malitza, 1979, p. 10). Maintenance learning reinforces the values of the system it is designed to maintain and ignores others.

   When values are in conflict, learning opportunities are present. For this reason values are called, 'the enzymes of any innovative learning process' (p. 40).

6. Although part of this final solution contained the well-established custom of a committee appointed by the larger body, this was not done, as is usually the case, to relieve the larger group of cumbersome discussions. The group had already heard the various sides of the problem and had experienced the 'loss of time' and circular confusion of such deliberations. Rather, the committee was formulated out of respect for the boy, so as not to paralyze him in a confrontation with a large and formidable group of adults. At the same time the committee truly represented those who felt strongly for each side of the dispute. Thus, it was a genuine confrontation of the group, not merely investigative. As the large group had thoroughly participated, it did not (as often happens in parliamentary bodies) have to cross-examine the committee's findings or second-guess its conclusions.

References

Allaway, A. J. (1971) *Exploring human behaviour in groups*. Tunbridge Wells, England: Institute for Cultural Research Monograph Series.

Barker, R.G. (1968) *Ecological psychology*. Stanford University Press.

Barrett-Lennard, G. T. (1977) *Toward a person-centered theory of community*. West Perth, Australia: Centre for Studies in Human Relations monograph.

Becker, E. (1969) *Angel in armor*. New York: George Brasiller.

Bortoft, H. (1996) *The wholeness of nature: Goethe's way of science*. New York: Floris Books.

Botkin, J.W., Elmandjra, M. and Malitza, M. (1979) *No limits to learning: Bridging the human gap*. Oxford: Pergamon Press.

Bowen, M., Miller, M., Rogers, C.R. and Wood, J.K. (1979) Learnings in large groups: Their implications for the future. *Education, 100* (2): 108–16.

Bowers, J.W. and Osborn, M.M. (1966) Attitudinal effects of selected types of concluding metaphors in persuasive speech. *Speech Monographs, 33*: 147–55.

Bozarth, J.D. (1982) The person-centered approach in the large community group. In G. Gazda (ed.) *Innovations in group psychotherapy*. 2nd Edition. Springfield Ilinois: Charles Thomas.

Bradford, C.P., Gibb, J.R. and Benne, K.D. (1964) *T-group theory and laboratory method*. New York: Wiley.

Brodeur, P. (1989) The hazards of electro-magnetic fields. *The New Yorker*. June 12–26. Three parts.

Buber, M. (1957) *Pointing the way*. New York: Harper and Row.

Buber, M. (1958) *I and thou*. New York: Scribner and Sons.

Buber, M. (1966) *The knowledge of man: A philosophy of the interhuman*. M.S. Friedman (ed.) New York: Harper and Row.

Colson, D.B. and Horwitz, L. (1983) Research in group psychotherapy. In H.I. Kaplan and B.J. Sadock (eds.) *Comprehensive group psychotherapy*. London: Williams and Wilkins. The authors cite a study by D. Malan at the Tavistok Clinic.

Doob, L.W. (1970) (ed.) *Resolving conflict in Africa: The Fermeda workshop*. The Yale University Press.

DuBos, R. (1981) *Celebrating life*. New York: McGraw Hill.

Dunbar, R.I.M. (1996) *Grooming, gossip, and the evolution of language*. Harvard University Press.

Freire, E. (1997) E-mail correspondence, September/November.

Hall, E.T. (1959) *The silent language*. New York: Doubleday.

Hall, E.T. (1966) *The hidden dimension*. New York: Doubleday.

Harris, M. (1989). *Our kind*. New York: Harper and Row.

Hirst, W., Niesser, U. and Spelke, E. (1978) Divided attention. *Human Nature, 1*, 54–61.

James, W. (1890) *The principles of psychology*. New York: Henry Holt.

James, W. (1896) *Exceptional mental states*. The Lowell Lectures. Edited by

Eugene Taylor. University of Massachusetts Press.

Keats, J. (1899) *The complete poetical works of Keats*. Boston: Houghton Mifflin.

Kreuger, A.P. and Reed, E.J. (1976) Biological impact of small air ions. *Science, 193*: 1209–13.

Lago, C. (1994) Personal communication. 17 May.

LeBon, G. (1895) *The crowd*.

MacMillan, M. and Lago, C. (1993) Large groups: Critical reflections and some concerns. *The Person-Centered Approach and Cross-Cultural Communication, 2*.

McIlduff, E. and Coghlan, D. (1989) Process facilitation in a cross-cultural communication workshop. *Person-Centered Review, 4* (1): 77–98.

McIlduff, E. and Coghlan, D. (1993) The cross-cultural communications workshops in Europe – reflections and review. *The Person-Centered Approach and Cross-Cultural Communication, 2*.

Merleau-Ponty, M. (1964) *Sense and non-sense*. Northwestern University Press.

Midgley, M. (1978) *Beast and man*. Cornell University Press.

Mintz, N.L. (1956) Effects of esthetic surroundings: II. Prolonged and repeated experiences of a 'beautiful' and an 'ugly' room. *The Journal of Psychology, 41*: 459–66.

Mithen, S. (1996) *The prehistory of the mind*. London: Thames and Hudson.

Nelson, A. (1977) Unpublished doctoral thesis. Harvard University.

Perelman, C. and Olbrechts-Tyeca, L. (1969) *The new rhetoric: A treatise on argumentation*. (J. Wilkinson and P. Weaver, Tr.) University of Notre Dame Press. Quoted in Shotter, J. (1995) In conversation. *Theory and Psychology, 5* (1): 49–73.

Rogers, C.R. (1955) Persons or science? A philosophical question. *The American Psychologist, 10* (7): 267–78.

Rogers, C.R. (1970) *On encounter groups*. New York: Harper and Row.

Rogers, C.R. (1974) Remarks on the future of client-centered therapy. In D.A. Wexler and L.N. Rice (eds.) *Innovations in client-centered therapy*. New York: John Wiley and Sons.

Rogers, C.R. (1980) *A way of being*. Boston: Houghton Mifflin.

Rogers, C.R. (1984) Building a person-centered approach to international disputes: A step in the practice of peace. Proposal for what would become the Rust Workshop. La Jolla, California: Center for Studies of the Person.

Rogers, C.R. (1985) A client-centered/person-centered approach to therapy. In I.L. Kutush and A. Wolf (eds.) *Psychotherapists casebook: Theory and technique in practice*. San Francisco: Jossey-Bass.

Rogers, C.R. (1986) The Rust workshop: A personal overview. *The Journal of Humanistic Psychology, 26* (3): 23–45.

Rogers, C.R., Wood, J.K., Nelson, A., Fuchs, N. and Meador, B. (1986) An experiment in self-determined fees. *Estudos de Psicologia, 3* (1 and 2): 5–22.

Rosenthal, N.E., et al., (1984) Seasonal affective disorder: A description of the syndrome and preliminary findings with light therapy. *Archives of General Psychiatry, 41*: 72–80.

Searles, J.R. (1995) *The construction of social reality*. New York: The Free Press.

Sheldrake, R. (1981) *A new science of life: The hypothesis of formative causation*. Los Angeles: J.P Tarcher.

Shor, R.E. (1959) Hypnosis and the concept of the generalized reality-orientation. *American Journal of Psychotherapy, 13*: 582–602.

Slack, S. (1985) Reflections on a workshop with Carl Rogers. *Journal of Humanistic Psychology, 25* (2): 35–42.

Wood, J.K. (1982) Person-centered group therapy. In G. Gazda (ed.) *Basic approaches to group psychotherapy and group counseling*. Springfield, Ilinois: Charles Thomas.

Wood, J.K. (1984) Communities for learning: A person-centered approach to large groups. In R. Levant and J. Shlien (eds.) *Client-centered therapy and the person-centered approach: New directions in theory, research and practice*. New York: Praeger.

Wood, J.K. (1994a) The person-centered approach's greatest weakness: Not using its strength. *The Person-Centered Journal, 1* (3): 96–105.

Wood, J.K. (1994b) A rehearsal for understanding the phenomenon of group. *The Person-Centered Journal, 1* (3): 18–32.

Wood, J.K. (1995) The person-centered approach: Toward an understanding of its implications. *The Person-Centered Journal, 2* (2): 18–35.

Wood, J.K. (1997) Notes on studying large group workshops. *The Person-Centered Journal, 4* (Fall): 65–77.

Yalom, I.D. (1985) *The theory and practice of group psychotherapy*. New York: Basic Books.

Experiences of Separateness and Unity in Person-Centred Groups

10

Alan Coulson

We are all like islands, separate at the surface but connected in the deep.

William James

Introduction

This chapter is based on experience of over twenty large residential multicultural workshops. They varied from seven to ten days in duration and from thirty-five to over a hundred and forty in number of participants. These events have minimal structure but the community meeting – the regular, at least daily, gathering of all participants – was the centrepiece of each workshop. The terms *workshop*, *group*, and *community* all refer here to meetings of the whole membership though these gatherings may not always be attended by every participant.

The community meeting is where the overall 'condition' of the workshop is most readily discernible and most keenly felt. However, every interaction during the workshop period whether it is in the large group arena or in smaller groupings, over meals or drinks, or sharing music and dancing, contributes to the experience of the individual and is integral to the life of the group. The smaller groupings, whether spontaneous (such as informal conversations) or arranged (such as subgroups and special interest groups), affect the atmosphere and coherence of the larger meeting when it reassembles.

There exist a number of hypotheses regarding the phases of group development (e.g., Tuckman, 1965; Schutz, 1979) and community creation (Peck, 1990). However, their sequential stages are of limited value in considering the person-centred workshop. Rogers (1980, p.189) commented, 'So complex is the process within these workshop groups that I despair of doing more than hinting at its multifaceted aspects'. According to Ruth Sanford (1993, p.267) the central problem is that of '. . . trying to build a step structure to express a fluid process'. Some commentators question whether there is a discernible group process at all (Bozarth,

1998a). Certainly, each participant is engaged in his or her own individual, subjective process, and accounts of perceptions and experiences reveal large differences (e.g., Wood, 1994; Bozarth, 1998b). Moreover, these large groups are complex and multifaceted. Thus at any time there may be a variety of processes, individual and collective, occurring.

Workshops may not necessarily give rise to the individual experiences and group phenomena described here. Nevertheless, many discussions with fellow-participants and written accounts (e.g., Wood, 1994) confirm that perceptions and experiences similar to my own are common. I believe, therefore, that these phenomena are present in most, if not all, large workshops and that a substantial proportion of workshop participants has had similar experiences.

I focus here upon just one significant theme which seems to me to have run through every workshop I have attended. On each occasion I have moved from initially feeling relatively separate and bounded, to a sense of being deeply connected with other people within the group and beyond it.

The person-centred workshop
Conditions of worth
The progression from experiencing separateness to experiencing connectedness or unity reflects the individual's transition from a self-concept governed by *conditions of worth*, accompanied by feelings of inhibition and defensiveness, to an expanded, more authentic notion of self in which there is a sense of greater authenticity and freedom.

Within the person-centred approach, *conditions of worth* (Rogers, 1959) is the central consideration in the development of the self-concept. Throughout a person's socialization, their 'worth' as defined by significant others, such as parents, teachers and peers, is dependent on whether they measure up to certain conditions. In other words, the person's sense of worth is conditional upon winning approval and avoiding disapproval. All of us have been subject to this process to some extent. However, where the conditions were particularly stringent and have been introjected, the person may have developed a semi-perpetual feeling of vulnerability for fear of 'getting it wrong'. Under these circumstances, part of the mind is continually on guard, watching and judging, constantly monitoring thought and constraining behaviour.

In broad terms then, the operation of the conditions of worth instilled by our upbringing and reinforced by the social environment may serve as a barrier restricting and confining us to a 'small' self, one which discourages creative interpersonal behaviour and spontaneous emotional expression. The person-centred community group can promote radical shifts of awareness and self-concept by providing a psychological environment in which external reinforcements of the conditions are removed. Instead, the group may foster change by providing a context in which persons are valued regardless of whether they meet the conditions of worth set out for them in their lives. Lietaer (1984) calls this process *counter-conditioning*.

Typically group members are relatively isolated from their usual surroundings, their families, and their customary social contacts. Instead of being within a familiar setting, dedicated to upholding conventional social expectations and maintaining a predictable structure, they are in one which encourages naturalness, spontaneity, and authenticity of expression. If the group develops an increasingly non-judgmental atmosphere, as most do, participants tend to feel increasingly accepted and self-accepting. Their confidence and trust grows and their self-concepts are enhanced.

From separateness to unity
At the beginning of a workshop I imagine that, like myself, many participants feel that they are surrounded largely by strangers – people who seem as separate as themselves and many of whom appear at first to be very different from them. By the end, however, I am in the company of people with at least some of whom I have shared intensely and intimately, and with whom I feel a close bond. For many of us the sense of unity or communion with other group members is one of the most deeply satisfying outcomes of participation in these workshops. Sometimes this feeling expands beyond the group to encompass a sense of connectedness with all humankind, with nature, or even with the whole universe. It seems that experience in a workshop may more clearly illuminate one's individual identity and at the same time one may be taken up into a new whole that is somehow larger than the self on its own. Of this experience Carl Rogers observed,

> Each individual tends to use the opportunity to become all that he or she *can* become. Separateness and diversity – the uniqueness of being 'me' are experienced. This very characteristic seems to raise the group level to a oneness of consciousness.

(Rogers, 1980, p. 190)

Normally, however, participants have realizations of this kind only in the later stages of the life of the workshop.

In a person-centred community many of the early interactions are characterised by the attempts of individuals to make themselves known and to make or find their place in the group. Some will give brief monologues of self-presentation, tell part of their 'story', or express their hopes and expectations. Others will be trying to 'shape' the workshop by making proposals about format or scheduling. Many participants find such a large gathering intimidating but feel they are not really present until they have spoken in the group, even if only to introduce themselves. Still others may begin to address the group at large, to share what they perceive to be happening, or to respond to previous contributions. The pace is often rapid and, especially in a very large meeting, it is difficult for some people to find a space in which to speak. Moreover, '. . . people speak disconnectedly from each other. Prepared statements are mingled with moving personal expressions of current feeling and there is no space for any response which takes time to form' (MacMillan and Lago, 1993, p.41).

During the opening phases of a community most of the issues and needs dealt with are pre-existing ones which we have imported into the workshop arena from our personal histories and cultural conditioning. This is, in effect, an aspect of our self-presentation for it is through sharing experiences, feelings, and reactions that we re-create the story we tell others – and ourselves – about who we are (Dennett, 1992).

As the group progresses, however, I find that I am focused less upon what I and others have brought with us but increasingly with how I am, and we are, *now*. My self-consciousness, and my fear of the group situation have by this time diminished. I seem to be thinking less about what is happening and my place in it; rather I am becoming more present, more open to what is occurring within myself and within the group *in the moment*. My thoughts and behaviour are beginning to escape from the control hitherto exerted by my conditions of worth. As I settle into the group I feel more connected with myself, more natural and spontaneous, less separate and more able to connect with others. It is as if I am going simultaneously *inward*, joining more with myself, and going *outward*, joining more with others. Another workshop participant expressed a similar feeling:

> We see ourselves reflected in the group that is a part of us, at the same time that we are a part of it. To be in contact with our own experiences is the same as to be in contact with the other or with the group since they make part of us.
>
> (Reported in Wood, 1994, p.27)

Usually, with the passage of time the community climate, though varying from meeting to meeting, feels safer and more accepting. Debates over matters of scheduling and organization usually persist well into the workshop. However, as it evolves, in-depth attention to individual issues and concerns becomes more prominent. In time, a slower rhythm evolves, '. . . individuals gradually begin to *hear* one another, and then slowly to understand and to respect' (Rogers, 1980, p.193). As people begin to feel more deeply heard, disclosure and feedback flow more freely. There is more genuine listening to *persons* rather than merely their words, illustrating Hayakawa's (1949) statement that 'the meanings of words are not in the words, they are in us'.

More contributions have a heartfelt quality and there is an increase in group coherence as members interact from deeper parts of themselves. Emotions frequently speak more directly across interpersonal boundaries than words. There is not necessarily widespread agreement about issues, but members' attunement to each other is growing and most people are increasingly sensitive in their interactions. A member of a workshop in Latin America wrote,

> It would be observed that many people showed an amazing amount of attention and solicitude towards others in the last few days. All this and much more give the group a distinctly different face from its initial one.
>
> (Quoted in Wood, 1994, p. 21)

A growing number of members begin to address topics relating to the group as a collectivity. Moreover, alongside the continuing struggles with interpersonal and emotional issues, consideration of existential and spiritual issues may appear, issues at a level which eludes explicit description – the 'tacit' level.

As the community develops, individuals occasionally become completely absorbed in the proceedings. They may become so wholeheartedly engaged, so open and present to the moment that their whole being is in an undivided state of extreme sensitivity. When individuals are functioning in this manner they often seem to speak less often. When they do their contributions are less prepared or self-monitored, and more spontaneous. When I have experienced this condition my self-consciousness, my internal monologue, even my thoughts and my sense of time all seem to be temporarily suspended. My self-created barriers are lowered, and the conditioned feeling of separateness they enclosed is set aside, leaving me feeling integrated and whole. In this 'self-forgetting', 'no-mind' quality of consciousness it is as if there is no separate self functioning apart from the organism; there is just experiencing, seeing and *being*. According to Lee (1998) such experiences involve the surrender of the imagined, fabricated existence of the self, revealing a deeper, internal Self, which is the same Self in all of us. The spontaneous laying aside of habitual and customary ways of relating and responding allows us to establish communion with one another without, as it were, the 'filters' of the conditioned self. Santos (1998) agrees that it is through entering into the non-ordinary state of consciousness of the Self that we can truly join with others.

Within the community an encounter of this profound, unconditional kind between members has a major impact on the group atmosphere. The powerful emotional quality of such interactions affects everyone present and tends to move individuals and the group towards a deeper level of functioning and, usually, a feeling of greater closeness.

Matters relating to the group as a collectivity intertwine with individual and interpersonal issues. Transpersonal and spiritual concerns make more frequent appearances. Participants' priorities do differ, however, and some discordance is often apparent among subgroups who are operating at different levels of concern. Nevertheless, if listening and caring are sensitive, the community may attain a harmonious way of working which can be multilayered and is satisfying to participants of differing perspectives.

The emergence of subtle transpersonal and transcendent considerations is normally accompanied by further changes in the dominant rhythm and verbal style of the group. Along with a general slowing down of pace there are frequently more and longer relaxed silences. It is as though members are now allowing contributions to sink in gradually, allowing their meaning to emerge gently and to be accepted or welcomed. There is less urgency to respond.

Finding issues and feelings at the tacit level difficult to express in straightforward prose, there is increasing resort to poetry (sometimes quoted, sometimes composed on the spot), to metaphor and imagery. The metaphorical language of poetry has the advantage that it goes beyond the words themselves to suggest the sensed and implicit actuality that hides behind the visible and tangible aspects of existence. Moreover, as Lancaster (1991, p. 183) explains, through the resonance of sound, rhythm and metaphor, poetry has the power '. . . to lead the mind into that state in which the inspiration was born'. Within the community the evolving feeling of mutuality and the sense of being part of something greater, more universal, may also be signalled in other ways. Members may draw closer physically, sitting in closer proximity to each other. Some people express themselves in drawing or singing, others through the exchange of smiles and gentle touch. Some may present a gift, flowers, for instance, to another participant or to the whole group. There is a noticeable relaxation of previous tensions and an air of quiet celebration. It feels as though having struggled through a long and difficult journey together the group has, temporarily anyway, arrived at a place of fulfilment and rest. Sometimes there remains only what Rogers (1980, p.196) called '. . . the presence of an almost telepathic communication'. The group may then fall silent, simply being together comfortably united in 'communion'.

One of Wood's (1994, p.21) respondents wrote:

The fact is it seemed the group had searched for a unity, that in my view can only be found when it transcends words . . . I noted that language was not very important when you really want to 'listen' to someone . . .

Another reported:

The silence that followed (an outburst of indignation) and the subsequent reflections by members of the group formed for me a genuine unity . . . It was as if all our consciousnesses were one thing only, alive and promising.

In the particular quality of silence with which a community is sometimes blessed, the atmosphere is pervaded by an intense and vibrant, yet relaxed stillness. In this stillness, group and individual, mind and body are no longer experienced as being divided one from another. The words of the Native American Black Elk indicate this state:

The first peace, which is most important, is that which comes within the souls of people when they realize their relationship, their oneness, with the universe and all its powers, and when they realize that at the center of the universe dwells the Great Spirit, and that this center is really everywhere, it is within each of us.

Facilitation or 'resonance': functioning from the Self

The issue of facilitation of person-centred groups has been explored by, among others, McIlduff and Coghlan (1989), Rogers (1970), Macmillan and Lago (1996) and Bozarth (1998b). I have suggested elsewhere (Coulson, 1994b) that the issue of group facilitation is problematic insofar as no one can predict who is going to do or say something which is facilitative for another.

Nor can one forecast what offerings contribute most fruitfully to the functioning of the group as a whole. The advantages and disadvantages of having designated facilitators are considered by MacMillan and Lago (1993, pp. 40–5) and Bozarth (1998b, 152–9).

In regard to the transition from experiences of separateness from others to experiences of feeling deeply connected with them, what I have chosen to call *resonance* is perhaps more important than *facilitation*. Because of the variety of people in a large workshop there are normally individuals who come to feel a special affinity with another participant's situation or to 'resonate' with them in such a way that one is facilitative to the other, either in the group meeting or in the larger arena of the workshop outside it. The bond may relate only to spontaneous participation in a particular episode in the group or it may become part of an ongoing special relationship. The basis of such a deep connection is frequently difficult to identify since its foundation may be at a level other than that of conscious awareness. It is likely, however, that the basis is an emotional connectedness within which those involved feel more deeply in touch with themselves than before and more closely linked with another. In effect the psychological boundary between two people has been breached, enabling something in one to reach deeply into the other. It could be said that in such a situation their contact is through the Self which is common to both.

In a community where freedom of expression exists, potentially there are many significant others to give acceptance and support. Even in a group which has designated facilitators, an individual may find that people other than facilitators are better suited or more equipped to render them support and encouragement. In any case, a climate pervaded by unconditional positive regard enables individuals to strengthen their own positive self-esteem. This permits them to loosen the hold over their thoughts and actions which may have been exercised by the conditional regard they were exposed to in early life and which has been sustained by social pressures.

Contributions in the group, especially those which are emotionally laden, may evoke a powerful resonance in another participant whose response is somehow 'just right' to facilitate the episode. These reactions or interventions often arise spontaneously from an unexpected quarter. The facilitating person has acted from a resonance or inner sense which may not be fully available to conscious awareness. I suspect that the resonance process differs somewhat from empathy as discussed in the context of person-centred therapy. Rather than entering the perceptual world of another or seeking deep non-judgmental understanding, resonance among group members refers to a feeling of connectedness through emotional affinity, frequently at a subconscious level. Understanding may develop and rise to conscious awareness later.

The spontaneous sharing of deeply personal issues may in itself ease the way for others to open up more or to deepen their level of responding. Amplifying his well-known comment, 'What is most personal is most general', Carl Rogers declared,

    . . . I have almost invariably found that the very feeling which has

> seemed to me most private, most personal and hence most incomprehensible by others, has turned out to be an expression for which there is a resonance in many other people. It has led me to believe that what is most personal and unique in each one of us is probably the very element which would, if it were shared or expressed, speak most deeply to others.
>
> (Rogers, 1961, p. 26)

Within the community group, expressions which have resonances for a variety of participants foster a greater sense of overall connectedness and a stronger communal feeling.

In workshops people often refer back to earlier comments or episodes. Though they have apparently not responded to these incidents at the time, something about them has struck a chord within, the significance of which has emerged later. On many occasions, of course, we say and do things in workshops, as in life, that assist others or provide them with insights, yet we remain quite unaware of it unless told subsequently. In many instances, then, facilitation is actually inadvertent. To sum up, it is proposed that a high proportion of effective 'facilitative' interventions are natural, spontaneous and, often, intuitive. Sometimes, as I have just indicated, they take the form of a contribution which has deep resonances for other participants. On other occasions they may have an even deeper source and be the result of profound merging of the consciousnesses of the individuals concerned. I believe it is probably this latter phenomenon to which Carl Rogers refers in his, now much-quoted, statement,

> When I am at my best, as a group facilitator or as a therapist, I discover another characteristic. I find that when I am closest to my inner, intuitive self, when I am somehow in touch with the unknown in me, when perhaps I am in a slightly altered state of consciousness, then whatever I do seems to be full of healing. Then, simply my *presence* is releasing and helpful to the other. There is nothing I can do to force this experience, but when I can relax and be close to the transcendental core of me, then I may behave in strange and impulsive ways in the relationship, ways which I cannot justify rationally, which have nothing to do with my thought processes. But these strange behaviours turn out to be *right* in some odd way: it seems that my inner spirit has reached out and touched the inner spirit of the other. Our relationship transcends itself and becomes a part of something larger. Profound growth and healing and energy are present.
>
> (Rogers, 1980, p.129)

Santos (1998, p.3) suggests that the phenomenon which Rogers describes here arises naturally and spontaneously on the rare occasions when we are operating from the (higher) *Self*. This is '. . . the self a person truly is'. He contends that when one is functioning from the Self, one will act from a place of peace within and everything one does will bring '. . . resolution, healing, learning, growth and development'.

In moments of resonance or profound contact with another in the community we may be functioning at this Self level, a level at which we are temporarily freed from the conditioning of our self-systems, our prescribed existences. The more group members express themselves from this unencumbered state, the more they are likely to experience relating without the blocks which customarily distance us one from another, and the more the group as a whole will feel unified.

Discussion

Throughout the ages, mystics and spiritual teachers of every cultural tradition have held that not only are all humans linked and interdependent, but that we, and everything else, are inseparable parts of a larger entity. This view that we are seamlessly part of the universe has found extensive confirmation from quantum theory (Bohm, 1980; Capra, 1975, 1997; Zohar and Marshall, 1994), cognitive science (Varela *et al*, 1991; Capra, 1997) and experimentation with altered states of consciousness (Grof, 1998). In fact, '. . . in a radically insightful way, science has made good the ancient intuition of the prophets' (Reanney, 1995b, p.35).

Having had very extensive experience of person-centred workshops, Bozarth (1998b) proposes that the powerful sense of *communion* they sometimes engender is related to the quantum concept of the universe as an interconnected web of relations, a dynamic, inseparable whole.

Within the workshop setting, the movement from feeling separate to feeling connected has been described in this chapter in terms of a shift from operating from the *self* to functioning from the *Self*. Deikman has clarified the relationship between the aspects of self as follows,

> The basic difference between Western psychology and the mystical
> tradition lies in our assumptions about the self. We regard the self as
> a type of object, localized to the body and separate from other objects;
> mysticism considers that belief to be an illusion because it applies
> only to a limited aspect of human life. Mystics insist there is a Self,
> masked by ordinary consciousness, unbound by space and time, that
> can be both individual and universal – as with the wave that exists
> and then merges completely with the ocean from which it has never
> been separated and whose substance is its own.
>
> (Deikman, 1982, p.63)

Peat (1987) suggests that '. . . the separation of an individual consciousness from that of the "group mind" of the tribe or social group is, historically speaking, relatively recent'. Many passages in the Old Testament, for example, move in a fluid way between speaking of the tribe and its individual representative without making any marked distinction between them. This suggests that such a differentiation was not secure.

In its origins, the content of consciousness is the whole world, but in

> the individual it becomes focused and concentrated, bound up with the individual's body and drawing upon various memories, habits, life experiences, and dispositions to result in a personal consciousness.
>
> (Peat, 1987, p.220)

In our daily social and working lives we normally think and behave as though we are clearly bounded, separate, and autonomous. Numerous seemingly obvious differences such as race, gender, age, and social status sustain the impression of separateness. Our attitudes and perceptions regarding our 'separate' nature have become so ingrained and taken for granted, that we are usually not consciously aware of them. However, the sense of universality in which an individual human being feels connected with all humanity remains a basic human experience, a part of a deeper personhood. Close involvement in a person-centred community holds the possibility of awakening us to a realization that our individual consciousness is integral to a much vaster system and that our potentialities are much greater than we imagine. Realizing more clearly the nature of the boundaries within which we have been operating, and discovering that they may be permeated or even dissolved is usually a liberating and joyful experience.

The development of language has been identified as the pivotal feature in the creation and maintenance of humankind's separate sense of self (Wilber, 1981; Reanney, 1995b). Our creation through language of the abstractions of separate objects, including a separate self, has led us to treat the natural environment and human society as if it consisted of separate parts.

> Our problem as human beings is that the very way our minds operate depends on the principle of separation . . . everything is divided by the very act that names it; the world is divided into mind and nature, the human is divided into body and soul, the territorial world is divided into a host of nations, the sacred sense is divided into a host of sects.
>
> (Reanney, 1995b, pp. 121–2)

It is significant that at the times when a person-centred community shows most harmony and unity there is a diminution in the employment of language in general, but more use of poetry and allusion. Often the deepest sensations of togetherness or communion are beyond words and result in silence and stillness. It seems that our words can often play a part in keeping us apart but moving back from them or going beyond them may reveal deeper, more subtle communication. In Herman Melville's words, 'All profound things and emotions of things are preceded and attended by silence'.

Even where an intellectual conviction exists that our separateness is an illusion, this runs counter to most people's habitual ways of perceiving, thinking, and behaving. Hence, before our underlying connectedness with others can be really deeply felt and become an integral part of our inner 'knowing', most of us have to have had an intense unitive experience. Unitive sensations take many different forms (Bucke, 1972). They may be brought on by drugs or long-distance running, for example, they may result from an overwhelming experience within natural surroundings, such as by the sea or on a mountain top, or arise through meditation, or, as is our concern here, through an intense experience within a group. Whatever their origin, they happen spontaneously and unbidden. The common factor among these experiences is an alteration in the state of consciousness to one of unusual sensitivity, receptiveness, and apparent clarity of awareness. These are usually accompanied by feelings of freedom and lightness. In this state the mind comes to rest so fully in the immediate experience that there is awareness of nothing else. The familiar conditions which structure ordinary consciousness are suspended.

Where the state of consciousness of a number of people within a workshop is involved, their individual self-systems seem to merge. A sense of underlying unity beneath their surface separation makes itself increasingly apparent. Both Bohm (1990) and O'Hara and Wood (1983) suggest that where a group displays a high degree of togetherness and coherence a form of group mind or collective consciousness is present. Bohm (p.14) calls it *participatory consciousness*. O'Hara and Wood suggest that:

> Individuals achieve integration with other group members and with the collective mind. The collective mind is also integrated within itself and within the larger world of which it is a part. In these moments of isomorphic integration the individual and the group gain access to a vastness of possibilities which is of cosmic proportions.
>
> (O'Hara and Wood, 1983, p.109)

It is clear that any feelings of differentiation and separation which may have existed in the groups to which Bohm, and O'Hara and Wood refer had been replaced by a sense of deep connectedness with other group members and, perhaps, beyond. As in the person-centred workshops I have attended, this process of integration is a transcendent experience which '. . . comes about spontaneously at times when we meet as persons on the different plane of our common humanity beyond all the divisions that ordinarily separate us' (Brink, 1987, p35).

A precondition for entry to the realm of the larger Self or participatory consciousness is the, usually involuntary, relinquishing of the control of the self-structure governed by the conditions of worth. This is, in effect, a process of surrender, surrender to a larger system, a larger configuration. Darryl Reanney (1995a, p. 246) has asserted that the true axis of human growth lies along the road that leads to the lowering of ego-boundaries. If this is so, for many of us, experience in the intensive person-centred workshop has sent us varying distances along that road. For some the collapse of long-established and firmly maintained ego-boundaries and a radical shift in consciousness amounts almost to the death of the pre-existing 'I' and the birth of a new more fully-functioning self/Self (Coulson, 1994a).

Conclusion

For many participants the person-centred group experience can lead to a greatly heightened sense of awareness and a much enhanced feeling both of self-worth and of interconnectedness with others (Thorne, 1992).

Most of us enter the large group experience thinking and acting very much in accordance with our conditioned and socially-shaped differences. It is the continual attention which we give to these differentiating factors which maintains our feeling of separateness and masks the commonality, the unity which lies beyond them. Immersion in the trust-building environment of the community offers an opportunity and an incentive for the self to put on one side its habitual preconceptions and responses. This process involves letting go of the controls which normally keep our conditioned ego-self in place, allowing a greater naturalness and spontaneity to flow. The relinquishing of our established identity means letting go of past conditioning and surrendering our familiar, self-protecting and limited way of being, for a leap of faith into experiencing more fully the present moment and the unity of the Self.

References

Bohm, David. (1980) *Wholeness and the Implicate Order.* London: Routledge and Kegan Paul.

Bohm, David. (1990) *On Dialogue.* Ohai, CA: David Bohm Seminars.

Bozarth, Jerold. (1985) Quantum Theory and the Person-Centred Approach. *Journal of Counselling and Development,* 64: 179–82.

Bozarth, Jerold. (1998a) Personal Communication, 16th September.

Bozarth, Jerold. (1998b) *Person-Centred Therapy: A Revolutionary Paradigm.* Ross-on-Wye: PCCS Books.

Brink, Debora C. (1987) The Issues of Equality and Control in the Client- or Person-Centred Approach. *Journal of Humanistic Psychology,* 27 (1), 27–37.

Bucke, Richard M. (1972) *Cosmic consiousness: a study in the evolution of the human mind.* Olympia Press: London. Originally published 1900.

Capra, Fritjof. (1975) *The Tao of Physics.* Shambhala: Boston.

Capra, Fritjof. (1997) *The Web of Life.* London: Flamingo.

Coulson, Alan. (1994a) Person-Centred Process and Personal Transformation. *Person Centred Practice,* 2, (1), 11–17.

Coulson, Alan. (1994b) Personal Communication cited in MacMillan and Lago, 1996, 604–5.

Deikman, A. (1982) *The Observing Self: Mysticism and Psychotherapy.* Boston: Beacon.

Dennett, Daniel. (1992) *Consciousness Explained.* London: Viking.

Grof, Stanislav. (1998) *The Cosmic Game: Explorations in the Frontiers of Human Consciousness.* Dublin: Newleaf.

Hayakawa, S.I. (1949) *Language in Thought and Action.* New York: Harcourt Brace.

Lancaster, Brian. (1991) *Mind, Brain and Human Potential.* Shaftesbury: Element.

Lee, Robert, E. (1998) Basic Encounter: Our Mutual Re-Search for Reality. Unpublished paper.

Lietaer, Germain. (1984) Unconditional Positive Regard: A Controversial Basic Attitude in Client-Centred Therapy, pp.41–58 in Levant, R. and J. Shlien (eds), *Client-Centred Therapy and the Person-Centred Approach*. New York: Praeger.

McIlduff, Edward and David Coghlan. (1989) Process and Facilitation in a Cross-Cultural Communication Workshop: Questions and Issues. *Person-Centred Review*, 4, (1), 77–98.

MacMillan, Mhairi and Colin Lago. (1993) Large Groups: Critical Reflections and Some Concerns. *The PCA and Cross-Cultural Communication: An International Review,* 11: 35–53.

MacMillan, Mhairi and Colin Lago. (1996) The Facilitation of Large Groups: Participants' Experiences of Facilitative Moments, in Hutterer, Robert *et al* (eds), *Client-Centred and Experiential Psychotherapy: A Paradigm in Motion*. Frankfurt: Peter Lang.

O'Hara, Maureen M. and John K. Wood. (1983) Patterns of Awareness: Consciousness and the Group Mind. *The Gestalt Journal*, 6, (2), 103–16.

Peat, F., David. (1987) *Synchronicity: The Bridge Between Matter and Mind*. New York: Bantam.

Peck, M.Scott. (1990) *The Different Drum*. London: Arrow.

Reanney, Darryl. (1995a) *The Death of Forever: A New Future for Human Consciousness*. London: Souvenir.

Reanney, Darryl. (1995b) *Music of the Mind: An Adventure into Consciousness*. London: Souvenir.

Rogers, Carl R. (1959) A Theory of Therapy, Personality, and Interpersonal Relationships, as Developed in the Client-Centred Framework, reprinted in Kirschenbaum, H. and V.L. Henderson (eds), *The Carl Rogers Reader.* London: Constable.

Rogers, Carl R. (1961) *On Becoming a Person*. London: Constable.

Rogers, Carl R. (1970) *Encounter Groups*. Harmondsworth: Penguin.

Rogers, Carl R. (1980) *A Way of Being*. Boston: Houghton Mifflin.

Sanford, Ruth. (1993) From Rogers to Gleick and Back Again, in Brazier, David (ed), *Beyond Carl Rogers*. London: Constable.

Santos, Antonio M. (1998) *The Person-Centred Approach – A New Formulation*, presentation to 7th International Forum for the Person-Centred Approach, Johannesburg, South Africa.

Schutz, Will. (1979) *Profound Simplicity*. New York: Bantam.

Thorne, Brian. (1992) *Carl Rogers*. London: Sage.

Tuckman, B.W. (1965) Developmental sequence in small groups. *Psychological Bulletin,* 63: 384–99.

Varela, Francisco, Evan Thompson and Eleanor Rosch. (1991) *The Embodied Mind*. Cambridge, Mass.: MIT Press.

Wilber, Ken. (1981) *Up from Eden: A Transpersonal View of Human Evolution*. Garden City, New York: Doubleday.

Wood, John K. (1994) A Rehearsal for Understanding the Phenomenon of Group. *The Person-Centred Journal,* 1, (3), 18–32.

Zohar, Dana and Ian Marshall. (1994) *The Quantum Society: Mind, Physics and a New Social Vision*. London: Flamingo.

INDEX OF NAMES

Also in this series

Person-Centred Approach
& Client-Centred Therapy
Essential Readers
Series editor Tony Merry

Person-Centred Therapy: *A Revolutionary Paradigm*

Jerold D. Bozarth

September 1998 ISBN 1 898059 22 5 234 x 156 pp 204 + vi £13.00.

Jerold D. Bozarth is Professor Emeritus of the University of Georgia, where his tenure included Chair of the Department of Counseling and Human Development, Director of the Rehabilitation Counseling Program and Director of the Person-Centered Studies Project. He is consultant for person-centred training programmes in the Czech Republic and Portugal; Scientific Director for the Person-Centred Learning Programme at the *Institute for Person-Centred Learning* in England; and is associated with the *Person Centred Connections* programme, also in England. He is currently researching working with individuals who have been considered 'impossible' by other helping organizations.

In this book Jerold Bozarth presents a collection of twenty revised papers and new writings on Person-Centred therapy representing over 40 years' work as an innovator and theoretician. Divided into five sections,
- Theory and Philosophy
- The Basics of Practice
- Applications of Practice
- Research
- Implications

this important book reflects upon Carl Rogers' theoretical foundations, emphasises the revolutionary nature of these foundations and offers extended frames for understanding this radical approach to therapy. This book will be essential reading for all with an interest in Client-Centred Therapy and the Person-Centred Approach.

• • •

Women Writers in the Person-Centred Approach

edited by Irene Fairhurst

September 1999 ISBN 1 898059 26 8 234 x 156 pp approx 190 £13.00

Edited by the co-founder of the British Association for the Person-Centred Approach (BAPCA), this book is the first anthology of women's writings informed by and focusing on the person-centred approach.

This uniquely themed collection includes contributions from all over the world, representing the wide range of developments in client-centred therapy and the person-centred approach.

PCCS Books was founded in 1993. We are a small publishing company specialising in books with a focus on the person-centred approach. We supply all major bookshops in the UK. Our books can be ordered direct from us via the contacts below. We ship worldwide direct to international customers – call for shipping costs.

PCCS Books, Llangarron, Ross-on-Wye, Herefordshire, HR9 6PT, United Kingdom
Telephone: +44 (0)1989 77 07 07   Fax: +44 (0)1989 77 07 00